The Citizen's Almanac

Fundamental

Documents, Symbols, and Anthems

of the United States

U.S. GOVERNMENT OFFICIAL EDITION NOTICE

AUTHENTICATED
U.S. GOVERNMENT
INFORMATION
GPO

Use of ISBN

This is the Official U.S. Government edition of this publication and is herein identified to certify its authenticity. Use of the ISBN 978-0-16-078003-5 is for U.S. Government Printing Office Official Editions only. The Superintendent of Documents of the U.S. Government Printing Office requests that any reprinted edition clearly be labeled as a copy of the authentic work with a new ISBN.

The information presented in *The Citizen's Almanac* is considered public information and may be distributed or copied without alteration unless otherwise specified. The citation should be:

U.S. Department of Homeland Security, U.S. Citizenship and Immigration Services, Office of Citizenship, *The Citizen's Almanac*, Washington, DC, 2007.

U.S. Citizenship and Immigration Services (USCIS) has purchased the right to use many of the images in *The Citizen's Almanac*. USCIS is licensed to use these images on a non-exclusive and non-transferable basis. All other rights to the images, including without limitation and copyright, are retained by the owner of the images. These images are not in the public domain and may not be used except as they appear as part of this publication.

For sale by the Superintendent of Documents, U.S. Government Printing Office
Internet: bookstore.gpo.gov   Phone: toll free (866) 512-1800;   DC area (202) 512-1800
Fax: (202) 512-2104 Mail: Stop IDCC, Washington, DC 20402-0001

ISBN 978-0-16-078003-5

Table of Contents

**U.S. Citizenship
and Immigration
Services**

Message from the Director

TODAY YOU ARE A CITIZEN OF THE UNITED STATES OF AMERICA—
becoming "a peer of kings" as President Calvin Coolidge once said. This
occasion is a defining moment that should not soon be forgotten, for it
marks the beginning of a new era in your lifetime as a U.S. citizen.

Naturalized citizens are an important part of our great democracy, bring-
ing a wealth of talent, ability, and character to this Nation. Your fellow
citizens recognize the sacrifices you have made to reach this milestone
and with open arms we welcome you. The United States offers an abun-
dance of freedom and opportunity for all its citizens and we wish you all
the best along the way.

As you will read in this booklet, *The Citizen's Almanac*, naturalized citizens
have played an important role in shaping this country. From Alexander
Hamilton to Albert Einstein, foreign-born Americans have contributed
to all aspects of society—literature, motion pictures, public service, and
athletics, to name just a few. As a citizen of the United States, it is now
your turn to add to this great legacy.

For more than 200 years, we have been bound by the principles and
ideals expressed in our founding documents, but it is up to citizens
like you to carry on this legacy for future generations.

Upon taking he Oath of Allegiance, you claimed for yourself the God-
given unalienable rights that the Declaration of Independence sets forth
as a natural right to all people. You also made a commitment to this
country and were therefore awarded its highest privilege—U.S. citizenship; but great responsibilities accompany this privilege. You now have
certain rights and responsibilities that you must exercise in order to

maintain our system of government. By becoming an active and participatory citizen, you further strengthen the foundation of our Nation.

The United States of America is now your country and *The Citizen's Almanac* contains information on the history, people, and events that have brought us where we are today as a beacon of hope and freedom to the world. We hope the contents of this booklet will serve as a constant reminder of the important rights and responsibilities you now have as a U.S. citizen. By continuing to learn about your new country, its founding ideals, achievements, and history, you will enjoy the fruits of responsible citizenship for years to come. Through your efforts, the freedom and liberty of future generations will be preserved and ensured.

May you find fulfillment and success in all your endeavors as a citizen of this great Nation. Congratulations and welcome. May the United States of America provide you peace, opportunity, and security.

Citizenship in America: Rights and Responsibilities of U.S. Citizens

All people in the United States have the basic freedoms and protections outlined in our founding documents, the Declaration of Independence and the Constitution. For more than 200 years, we have been bound by the ideals expressed in these documents. Because of these ideals, our society has prospered. The U.S. government, as established in the Constitution, protects the rights of each individual, without

> "We hold these truths to be self-evident, that all men are created equal, that they are endowed by their Creator with certain unalienable Rights, that among these are Life, Liberty and the Pursuit of Happiness."
>
> — Declaration of Independence

Adopted son of a U.S. service-man becomes a U.S. citizen in U.S. District Court, Madison, WI, May 28, 1971.

Photo taken by L. Roger Turner, Wisconsin State Journal, courtesy of the USCIS Historical Library

Early 20th century immigrants.

Courtesy of the USCIS Historical Library

regard to background, culture, or religion. To keep our system of representative democracy and individual freedom, you should strive to become an active participant in American civic life.

When you took the Oath of Allegiance, you promised your loyalty and allegiance to the United States of America. You now have other rights and responsibilities only given to United States citizens. These include the right to vote in federal elections and the ability to serve on a jury. Citizenship is a privilege that offers you the extraordinary opportunity to be a part of the governing process. The strength of the United States is in the will of its citizens.

Former Supreme Court Justice Louis Brandeis once said, "The only title in our democracy superior to that of President [is] the title of citizen." In the United States, the power of government comes directly from people like you. To protect freedom and liberty, U.S. citizens must participate in the democratic process and in their communities. The following is a

list of some of the most important rights and responsibilities that all citizens should exercise and respect. We encourage you to read the Constitution to learn more about all of the rights and responsibilities of United States citizenship.

Rights of a Citizen

★ **Freedom to express yourself.**

"Freedom of expression" includes several individual rights. It includes freedom of speech, freedom to peaceably assemble, and the freedom to petition the government for a redress of grievances. In a representative democracy, individual beliefs and opinions are important to our national dialogue and necessary to maintain a responsible citizenry. Americans can speak and act as they wish as long as it does not endanger others or obstruct another's freedom of expression in the process.

In 1963, nearly 250,000 people gathered in Washington, DC, to speak out against segregation and petition for equal rights for all Americans.
Courtesy of the Library of Congress, LC-U9-10363-5

★ **Freedom to worship as you wish.**

In the United States, the freedom to hold any religious belief, or none at all, is considered a basic, or unalienable right. The government cannot violate this right. Religious intolerance is unacceptable in a society where everyone has individual freedom. In cases where religious practices hurt the common good or endanger the health of others, the Supreme Court has imposed minor limitations on the way some religious practices are performed.

★ Right to a prompt, fair trial by jury.

People accused of a crime have the right to a speedy and fair trial by a jury of peers. In a free society, those accused of a crime are assumed innocent until proven guilty in a court of law. The American system of justice treats all people fairly, ensuring the rights of the individual are maintained.

★ Right to keep and bear arms.

The Constitution protects the rights of individuals to have firearms for personal defense. This privilege is subject to reasonable restrictions designed to prevent unfit persons, or those with the intent to criminally misuse guns or other firearms, from obtaining such items.

★ Right to vote in elections for public officials.

By voting in federal, state, and local elections, citizens choose their government leaders. The right to vote is one of the most important liberties granted to American citizens. It is the foundation of a free society.

★ Right to apply for federal employment.

Public service is a worthy endeavor and can lead to an extremely rewarding career working for the American people. Many federal government jobs require applicants to have U.S. citizenship. As a U.S. citizen, you can apply for federal employment within a government agency or department.

★ Right to run for elected office.

U.S. citizenship is required for many elected offices in this country. Naturalized U.S. citizens can run for any elected office they choose with the exception of President and Vice President of the United States, which require candidates to be native-born citizens.

★ Freedom to pursue "life, liberty, and the pursuit of happiness."

As a society based on individual freedom, it is the inherent right of all Americans to pursue "life, liberty, and the pursuit of happiness." The United States is a land of opportunity. People are able to choose their

own path in life based on personal goals and objectives. Americans can make their own decisions and pursue their own interests as long as it does not interfere with the rights of others.

RESPONSIBILITIES OF A CITIZEN

★ **Support and defend the Constitution against all enemies, foreign and domestic.**

The Constitution establishes the U.S. system of representative democracy and outlines the inherent principles of freedom, liberty, and opportunity to which all citizens are entitled. The continuity of this Nation's unique freedoms depends on the support of its citizens. When the Constitution and its ideals are challenged, citizens must defend these principles against all adversaries.

Until 1920, women were not allowed to vote in political elections. This image shows two women, known as suffragettes, petitioning for the right to vote (ca. 1917) in New York State.

Courtesy of the Library of Congress, LC-USZ62-53202

A citizen casts his vote in Barnesville, MD, 1944.

★ **Stay informed of the issues affecting your community.**

Before casting your vote in an election, be sure to gain information about the issues and candidates running for office. Staying informed allows citizens the opportunity to keep the candidates and laws responsive to the needs of the local community.

★ **Participate in the democratic process.**

Voting in federal, state, and local elections is the most important responsibility of any citizen. Voting ensures that our system of government is maintained and individual voices are clearly heard by elected officials.

★ **Respect and obey federal, state, and local laws.**

Laws are rules of conduct that are established by an authority and followed by the community to maintain order in a free society. Every person living in the United States must follow laws established through federal, state, and local authorities.

★ **Respect the rights, beliefs, and opinions of others.**

Though the United States is a nation of diverse backgrounds and cultures, our common civic values unite us as one nation. Tolerance, through courtesy and respect for the beliefs and opinions of others, is the hallmark of a civilized society and ensures the continuity of liberty and freedom for future generations.

Red Cross volunteer poster, 1917.

★ **Participate in your local community.**

Being a responsible member of one's local community is important to the success of representative democracy. Community engagement through volunteerism, participation in town hall meetings and public hearings, joining a local parent-teacher association, and running for public office are ways individuals can actively contribute to the well-being of the community.

★ **Pay income and other taxes honestly, and on time, to federal, state, and local authorities.**

Taxes pay for government services for the people of the United States. Some of these services include: educating children and adults, keeping our country safe and secure, and providing medical services to the elderly and less fortunate. Paying taxes on time and in full ensures that these services continue for all Americans.

★ **Serve on a jury when called upon.**

Serving on a jury is a very important service to your community. In the United States, the Constitution guarantees that all persons accused of a crime have the right to a "speedy and public trial by an impartial jury." Jury service gives you the opportunity to participate in the vital task of achieving just, fair results in matters that come before the court.

Volunteers tutoring children at the South Baton Rouge Community Development Association in Louisiana, 1986.

Courtesy of the Corporation for National and Community Service

During World War I, 300 soldiers from Camp Upton in New York take the Oath of Allegiance as a result of a law granting U.S. citizenship to immigrants in the Armed Forces.

Courtesy of the USCIS Historical Library

★ Defend the country if the need should arise.

The Armed Forces of the United States, the military, is currently an all-volunteer force. However, should the need arise in time of war, it is important that all citizens join together and assist the Nation where they are able. This support could include defending the Nation through military, noncombatant, or civilian service.

A World War II B-24 bomber crew at their base in Nadzab, New Guinea, following a mission in 1944.

Courtesy of the Maloney family

Patriotic Anthems and Symbols of the United States

Beginning early in our Nation's history, citizens have used songs, poems, and symbols to express the ideals and values of the United States. From solemn oaths, such as the Pledge of Allegiance and the Oath of Allegiance, which one must take to become a citizen, to the more informal tradition of singing "The Star-Spangled Banner" before sporting events, spoken expressions have always been an important part of American civic life. As you will learn in this section, these songs and poems often came from a writer's personal interpretation of America's ideals, as with the story of Emma Lazarus and "The New Colossus."

The values and history of the United States are also expressed through visual symbols, such as the Great Seal of the United States and the Flag of the United States of America. Around the world, these two emblems are used to symbolize our solidarity as a nation. As a U.S. citizen, you can take pride in these symbols and the fact that they represent you and your country. The following section will introduce you to the history and meaning behind some of our most important patriotic anthems and symbols.

The Star-Spangled Banner (1814)
by Francis Scott Key

"The Star-Spangled Banner" is the national anthem of the United States. It was written by Francis Scott Key after a critical battle in the War of 1812. Key, a lawyer and amateur poet, had been sent to Baltimore, Maryland, to secure the release of Dr. William Beanes, an American taken prisoner by the British.

"The Star-Spangled Banner," the flag that inspired the national anthem.

Courtesy of the National Museum of American History, Smithsonian Institution

Boarding a British ship for the negotiations, Key was treated with respect by the British officers who agreed to release Dr. Beanes. Although the mission was completed, the British were about to attack Fort McHenry, the American fort guarding Baltimore, and so they did not allow the Americans to return to shore. For twenty-five hours, British

In "The Star Spangled Banner," a painting by Percy Moran, Francis Scott Key reaches out towards the flag flying over Fort McHenry. Courtesy of the Library of Congress, LC-USZ62-1764

gunboats shelled Fort McHenry. The Americans withstood the attack, and on the morning of September 14, 1814, Key peered through clearing smoke to see an enormous American flag waving proudly above the fort. Key was so inspired by this sight of the American flag that he began a poem to commemorate the occasion. He wrote the poem to be sung to the popular British song, "To Anacreon in Heaven."

The significance and popularity of the song spread across the

United States. In 1916, President Woodrow Wilson ordered that the song be played at military and naval occasions. In 1931, "The Star-Spangled Banner" became the official national anthem of the United States.

The Star-Spangled Banner

Oh, say, can you see, by the dawn's early light,

What so proudly we hailed at the twilight's last gleaming?

Whose broad stripes and bright stars, thro' the perilous fight;

O'er the ramparts we watched, were so gallantly streaming.

And the rockets red glare, the bombs bursting in air,

Gave proof through the night that our flag was still there.

Oh, say, does that star-spangled banner yet wave

O'er the land of the free and the home of the brave?

America the Beautiful
by Katharine Lee Bates (1893)

"America the Beautiful" was written in 1893 by Katharine Lee Bates, a professor of English literature at Wellesley College in Massachusetts. Bates wrote the lyrics while on a trip to Colorado Springs, Colorado. Describing the extraordinary view at the top of Pike's Peak she said, "It was then and there, as I was looking out over the sea-like expanse of fertile country spreading away so far under those ample skies, that the opening lines of the hymn floated into my mind."

On July 4, 1895, "America the Beautiful" first appeared in print in the *Congregationalist*, a weekly journal. A few months later, the lyrics were set to music by Silas G. Pratt. Bates revised the lyrics in 1904 after receiving many requests to use the song in publications and special services. In 1913, Bates made an additional change to the wording of the third verse, creating the version we know today.

For several years, "America the Beautiful" was sung to just about any popular or folk tune that would fit with the lyrics. In 1926, the National Federation of Music Clubs held a contest to put the

The view from Pike's Peak, which inspired the writing of "America the Beautiful."
Courtesy of the Library of Congress,
LC-DIG-stereo-1s01262

poem to music, but failed to select a winner. Today, "America the Beautiful" is sung to Samuel A. Ward's 1882 melody "Materna."

AMERICA THE BEAUTIFUL

O beautiful for spacious skies,
For amber waves of grain,
For purple mountain majesties
Above the fruited plain.
America! America! God shed His grace on thee,
And crown thy good with brotherhood
From sea to shining sea.

O beautiful for pilgrim feet,
Whose stern impassion'd stress
A thoroughfare for freedom beat
Across the wilderness.
America! America! God mend thine ev'ry flaw,
Confirm thy soul in self-control,
Thy liberty in law.

O beautiful for heroes prov'd
In liberating strife,
Who more than self their country loved,
And mercy more than life.
America! America! May God thy gold refine
Till all success be nobleness,
And ev'ry gain divine.

O beautiful for patriot dream
That sees beyond the years.
Thine alabaster cities gleam,
Undimmed by human tears.
America! America! God shed his grace on thee,
And crown thy good with brotherhood
From sea to shining sea.

God Bless America
by Irving Berlin (1938)

Irving Berlin, a Russian immigrant who became a naturalized U.S. citizen in 1918, wrote the song "God Bless America" while serving in the U.S. Army. Originally composed for a musical revue, Berlin made a few slight alterations to the lyrics and introduced the song in 1938. Singer Kate Smith sang the song for the first time to a national audience during her radio broadcast on November 11, 1938, in honor of Armistice Day (now Veterans Day). The song became popular almost immediately, and soon after its introduction, Berlin

Boy and Girl Scouts march in an Armistice Day parade, 1940. Courtesy of the LOC, LC-USF33-020711-M1

established the God Bless America Fund with which he dedicated the royalties from the song to the Boy and Girl Scouts of America. "God Bless America" is recognized today as America's unofficial national anthem.

GOD BLESS AMERICA

While the storm clouds gather far across the sea,
Let us swear allegiance to a land that's free,
Let us all be grateful for a land so fair,
As we raise our voices in a solemn prayer.

God Bless America.
Land that I love.
Stand beside her, and guide her
Thru the night with a light from above.
From the mountains, to the prairies,
To the oceans, white with foam
God Bless America.
My home sweet home.

I Hear America Singing

From Leaves of Grass
(1860 Edition)
by Walt Whitman

Walt Whitman, who lived from 1819 to 1892, is one of the most influential and beloved of American poets. As a young man, Whitman worked as a teacher in one-room schools on Long Island, New York. He taught until 1841 when he decided to begin a full-time career in journalism. Whitman established the *Long-Islander*, a weekly newspaper in New York, and often edited other newspapers in the surrounding area. He also spent time in New Orleans, Louisiana, and Washington, DC. By traveling to different cities in the United States, Whitman was exposed to how Americans lived in a variety of places. These experiences provided inspiration for some of Whitman's famous poems about his fellow countrymen, including "I Hear America Singing."

This poem was included in Whitman's

Walt Whitman.
Courtesy of the Library of Congress, LC-DIG-ppmsca-07549

most cherished work, the poetry collection, *Leaves of Grass*. Throughout his life, Whitman produced several editions of *Leaves of Grass*, a varied collection that began with only twelve poems in the 1855 first edition and contained nearly four hundred poems by the time the final edition was published in 1891. "I Hear America Singing," a celebration of the American people, was added to the collection in 1860.

I HEAR AMERICA SINGING

I hear America singing, the varied carols I hear,

Those of mechanics, each one singing his as it should be blithe and strong,

The carpenter singing his as he measures his plank or beam,

The mason singing his as he makes ready for work, or leaves off work,

The boatman singing what belongs to him in his boat, the deckhand
singing on the steamboat deck,

The shoemaker singing as he sits on his bench, the hatter singing as he stands,

The wood-cutter's song, the ploughboy's on his way in the morning, or
at noon intermission or at sundown,

The delicious singing of the mother, or of the young wife at work, or of the girl sewing
or washing,

Each singing what belongs to him or her and to none else,

The day what belongs to the day—at night the party of young fellows,
robust, friendly,

Singing with open mouths their strong melodious songs.

Concord Hymn (1837)
by Ralph Waldo Emerson

Ralph Waldo Emerson was a celebrated American author, poet, philosopher, and public speaker. He became the leader of a famous intellectual movement known as transcendentalism. Emerson had strong ties to the beginning of America's fight for independence. His grandfather was present at the opening battle of the American Revolution, the Battle of Lexington and Concord, in Massachusetts on April 19, 1775. His family home was also located next to the battlefield site.

The Obelisk at the battlefield in Concord, MA (ca.1900).
Courtesy of the Library of Congress, LC-D4-11872

"Concord Hymn" was written originally as a song for the dedication of the Obelisk, a monument commemorating the valiant effort of those who fought in the Battle of Lexington and Concord. The gunshot which began this battle is considered the beginning of America's fight for independence, and is referred to by Emerson as "the shot heard round the world." This phrase has since become famous and is often used in discussions of the American Revolution.

Ralph Waldo Emerson.
Courtesy of the Library of Congress, LC-USZ61-279

Concord Hymn

By the rude bridge that arched the flood,
Their flag to April's breeze unfurled,
Here once the embattled farmers stood,
And fired the shot heard round the world.

The foe long since in silence slept;
Alike the conqueror silent sleeps;
And Time the ruined bridge has swept
Down the dark stream which seaward creeps.

On this green bank, by this soft stream,
We set to-day a votive stone;
That memory may their deed redeem,
When, like our sires, our sons are gone.

Spirit, that made those heroes dare
To die, and leave their children free,
Bid Time and Nature gently spare
The shaft we raise to them and thee.

The New Colossus (1883)
by Emma Lazarus

As part of an auction held in 1883 to raise funds for a pedestal to be placed beneath the Statue of Liberty, which was a gift to America from France as part of the centennial celebration of 1876, Emma Lazarus wrote "The New Colossus." Her poem spoke to the millions of immigrants who came to America in search of freedom and opportunity. She saw the new statue as a symbol of hope and an inspiration to the world. In 1902, the poem was engraved on a bronze plaque at the base of the Statue of Liberty.

Inauguration of the Statue of Liberty in 1886, partly clouded by smoke from a military and naval salute marking President Grover Cleveland's arrival at the ceremony.
Courtesy of the Library of Congress, LC-USZ62-19869A

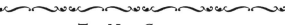

THE NEW COLOSSUS

Not like the brazen giant of Greek fame,
With conquering limbs astride from land to land;
Here at our sea-washed, sunset gates shall stand
A mighty woman with a torch, whose flame
Is the imprisoned lightning, and her name
Mother of Exiles. From her beacon-hand
Glows world-wide welcome; her mild eyes command
The air-bridged harbor that twin cities frame.
"Keep, ancient lands, your storied pomp!" cries she
With silent lips. "Give me your tired, your poor,
Your huddled masses yearning to breathe free,
The wretched refuse of your teeming shore.
Send these, the homeless, tempest-tost to me,
I lift my lamp beside the golden door!"

Flag of the United States of America

As America fought for its independence from Great Britain, it soon became evident that the new nation needed a flag of its own to identify American forts and ships. A design

The flag that was authorized by Congress on June 14, 1777.

of thirteen alternating red and white stripes and thirteen stars in a blue field was accepted by the Continental Congress on June 14, 1777. These stars and stripes honored the thirteen states that had joined together to form the United States of America.

As the United States expanded, however, more states were added to the Union. To celebrate the Nation's growth, Congress decided that the flag should become a visible symbol of change and established that the American flag would have one star for every state. The design of the American flag has changed twenty-seven times, and since 1959 it has had fifty stars and thirteen stripes.

The American flag is called the "Star-Spangled Banner," the "Stars and Stripes," the "Red,

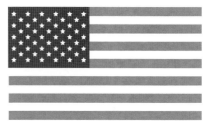

The U.S. flag today.

White, and Blue," and "Old Glory." To emphasize the importance of the American flag to the Nation and its people, Congress established June 14 of each year as Flag Day. On this day, Americans take special notice of the flag and reflect on its meaning.

Pledge of Allegiance

The Pledge of Allegiance was first published on September 8, 1892, in the *Youth's Companion* magazine. The original pledge read as follows, "I pledge allegiance to my Flag and the Republic for which it stands: one Nation indivisible, with Liberty and Justice for all." Children in public schools across the country recited the pledge for the first time on October 12, 1892, as part of official Columbus

Students recite the Pledge of Allegiance in a Washington, DC, classroom (ca. 1899).
Courtesy of the Library of Congress, LC-USZ62-14693

Citizens of Vale, OR, take off their hats during the Pledge of Allegiance, July 4, 1941.
Courtesy of the Library of Congress, LC-USF33-013070-M2

Day observances to celebrate the 400th anniversary of his discovery of America.

In 1942, by an official act, Congress recognized the pledge. The phrase "under God" was added to the pledge by another act of Congress on June 14, 1954. Upon signing the legislation to authorize the addition, President Dwight D. Eisenhower said, "In this way we are reaffirming the transcendence of religious faith in America's heritage and future; in this way we shall constantly strengthen those spiritual weapons which forever will be our country's most powerful resource in peace and war."

When delivering the Pledge of Allegiance, all must be standing at attention, facing the flag with the right hand over the heart. Men not in uniform should remove any nonreligious headdress with their right hand and hold it at the left shoulder, the hand being over the heart. Those in uniform should remain silent, face the flag, and render the military salute.

PLEDGE OF ALLEGIANCE

I pledge allegiance
to the Flag
of the United States of America
and to the Republic
for which it stands,
one Nation,
under God,
indivisible,
with liberty
and justice for all.

Great Seal
of the United States

On July 4, 1776, the Continental Congress appointed a committee to create a seal for the United States of America. Following the appointment of two additional committees, each building upon the other, the Great Seal was finalized and approved on June 20, 1782.

Obverse side of the Great Seal of the United States. *Courtesy of the U.S. Department of State*

The Great Seal has two sides—an obverse, or front side, and a reverse side. The obverse side displays a bald eagle, the national bird, in the center. The bald eagle holds a scroll inscribed *E pluribus unum* in its beak. The phrase means "out of many, one" in Latin and signifies one nation that was created from thirteen separate colonies. In one of the eagle's claws is an olive branch and in the other is a bundle of thirteen arrows. The olive branch signifies peace and the arrows signify war.

A shield with thirteen red and white stripes covers the eagle's breast. The eagle alone supports the shield to signify that Americans should rely on their own virtue and not that of other nations. The red and white stripes of the shield represent the states united under and supporting the blue, representing the President and Congress. The color red which form a constellation. The constellation represents the fact that the new Nation is taking its place among the sovereign powers.

The reverse side contains a thirteen-step pyramid with the year 1776 in Roman numerals at its base. Above the pyramid is the Eye of Providence and the motto *Annuit Coeptis*, meaning "He [God] favors our undertakings." Below the pyramid, *Novus Ordo Seclorum*, meaning "New Order of the Ages," is written on a scroll to signify the beginning of the new American era.

Reverse side of the Great Seal of the United States. Courtesy of the U.S. Department of State

signifies valor and bravery, the color white signifies purity and innocence, and the color blue signifies vigilance, perseverance, and justice. Above the eagle's head is a cloud that surrounds a blue field containing thirteen stars,

The obverse side of the Great Seal is used on postage stamps, military uniforms, U.S. passports, and above the doors of U.S. embassies worldwide. Both sides are present on the one dollar bill.

Motto of the United States

On July 30, 1956, President Dwight D. Eisenhower approved a Joint Resolution of the 84th Congress officially establishing the phrase, "In God We Trust," as the national motto of the United States. "In God We Trust" replaced the phrase, *E Pluribus Unum*, which had been selected as the Nation's official motto in 1776.

The motto, "In God We Trust," can be traced back nearly 200 years in U.S. history. During the War of 1812, as the morning light revealed that the American flag was still waving above Fort McHenry, Francis Scott Key wrote the poem that would eventually become our national anthem. The final stanza of the poem read, "And this be our motto: 'In God is our trust!'"

In 1864, Key's phrase was changed to "In God We Trust" and included on the redesigned two-cent coin. The following year, Congress authorized the Director of the Philadelphia Mint to place the motto on all gold and silver coins. The motto began appearing on all U. S. coins in 1938. "In God We Trust" became a part of the design of U. S. currency (paper money) in 1957. The Bureau of Engraving and Printing has incorporated the motto on all currency since 1963.

"In God We Trust" is also engraved on the wall above the Speaker's dais in the Chamber of the House of Representatives and over the entrance to the Chamber of the Senate.

President Lyndon B. Johnson delivering his State of the Union address before a joint session of Congress, January 8, 1964. Engraved above the Speaker's dais is the motto "In God We Trust."

Courtesy of the Lyndon Baines Johnson Library and Museum

Presidential and Historical Speeches

People in the United States greatly value their current and historical leaders. Following our democratic tradition, these leaders are remembered not only for their actions, but also for their speeches and proclamations to the American people. Beginning with President George Washington's call for unity in his 1796 Farewell Address, American leaders often emphasized similar themes when addressing the Nation.

President Abraham Lincoln perhaps best expressed the concept of unity and a common civic identity during the American Civil War, when our Nation's unity was severely threatened. Lincoln's speeches are also famous for referring to America, with its values and democratic system, as an important example for the rest of the world.

Much later, Presidents Franklin D. Roosevelt and John F. Kennedy called upon these same ideas in important speeches during times of crisis, and President Ronald Reagan was clearly inspired by these principles in his call for freedom around the world during the Cold War. In this section, you will also read about a leader who, rather than looking outside our borders, called on America itself to live up to its promise as a land of liberty and equality.

Farewell Address (1796)
George Washington

After leading the Continental army to victory over the British during the American Revolution, George Washington was the obvious choice to become the first president of the United States. Known as the "Father of Our Country," Washington performed honorably during his two terms as president in helping form the new government and guiding the young country through several foreign and domestic crises. Early in the year 1796, Washington decided not to seek reelection for a third time and began drafting a farewell address to the American people.

With the help of Treasury Secretary Alexander Hamilton, Washington completed his farewell address and the final version was printed in Philadelphia's *American Daily Advertiser* on September 19, 1796. Washington was concerned that increasing geographical sectionalism and the rise of political factions would threaten the stability of the eight-year-old Constitution and he used his address to urge Americans to unite for the long-term success of the Nation. He called for a distinctly "American character" that concentrated on the good of the country and would avoid potentially troublesome alliances with foreign nations.

On February 22, 1862, when America was engulfed in the Civil War, both houses of the U.S. Congress agreed to assemble and read aloud Washington's Farewell

"Washington Crossing the Delaware," by Emanuel Leutze.
Courtesy of the National Archives, NARA File # 066-G-15D-25

Address. This practice was later revived and performed annually by both houses of Congress. Since 1893, the U.S. Senate has observed our first president's birthday by selecting one of its members to read aloud Washington's Farewell Address from the Senate floor.

"George Washington at Princeton,"
by Charles Willson Peale.

EXCERPTS

...Citizens, by birth or choice, of a common country, that country has a right to concentrate your affections. The name of American, which belongs to you in your national capacity, must always exalt the just pride of patriotism, more than any appellation derived from local discriminations. With slight shades of difference, you have the same religion, manners, habits and political principles. You have in a common cause, fought and triumphed together; the independence and liberty you possess are the work of joint councils and joint efforts, of common dangers, sufferings, and successes....

It is substantially true, that virtue or morality is a necessary spring of popular government. The rule, indeed, extends with more or less force to every species of free government. Who that is a sincere friend to it can look with indifference upon attempts to shake the foundation of the fabric?

Promote, then, as an object of primary importance, institutions for the general diffusion of knowledge. In proportion as the structure of a government gives force to public opinion, it is essential that the public opinion should be enlightened.

First Inaugural (1861) Address

Abraham Lincoln

Abraham Lincoln was sworn in as the 16th president of the United States on March 4, 1861. This was a difficult time in our Nation's history. The issues of how much control the federal government should have over the states and whether to permit slavery in the newly acquired western territories divided the Union. In December 1860, shortly after Lincoln's election was declared final, the state of South Carolina seceded from the Union. By February 1861, six additional states seceded and formed the Confederate States of America under provisional president Jefferson Davis.

In an effort to calm the fears of the Southern states, Lincoln turned to four historic documents when preparing his inaugural remarks. Each of these references were concerned with states' rights: Daniel Webster's 1830 reply to Robert Y. Hayne; President Andrew Jackson's Nullification Proclamation of 1832; Henry Clay's compromise speech of 1850; and the Constitution of the United States. Lincoln believed that secession was illegal, and as chief executive, it was his responsibility to preserve the Union. The resulting speech was a message of unity to a troubled nation.

President Abraham Lincoln.
Courtesy of the National Archives, NARA File # 111-B-3656

Inauguration of President Abraham Lincoln on the steps of the U.S. Capitol, March 4, 1861.

EXCERPTS

...By the frame of the government under which we live, this same people have wisely given their public servants but little power for mischief; and have, with equal wisdom, provided for the return of that little to their own hands at very short intervals. While the people retain their virtue and vigilance, no administration, by any extreme of wickedness or folly, can very seriously injure the government in the short space of four years....

I am loath to close. We are not enemies, but friends. We must not be enemies. Though passion may have strained, it must not break our bonds of affection. The mystic chords of memory, stretching from every battle-field, and patriot grave, to every living heart and hearth-stone, all over this broad land, will yet swell the chorus of the Union, when again touched, as surely they will be, by the better angels of our nature.

Gettysburg Address (1863)
Abraham Lincoln

Considered one of the most important speeches in American history, Abraham Lincoln's Gettysburg Address successfully expressed the principles of liberty and equality that the United States was founded upon and proudly honored those that fought and perished for the survival of the Union. During his remarks, he spoke of "a new birth of freedom" for the Nation. Lincoln delivered this speech at the dedication of the Soldiers' National Cemetery at Gettysburg on November 19, 1863. The entire speech lasted just two minutes.

The Battle of Gettysburg took place July 1-3, 1863, in the rural town of Gettysburg, Pennsylvania, roughly 50 miles northwest of Baltimore, Maryland. Confederate forces, led by General Robert E. Lee's Army of Northern Virginia invaded Union territory, seeking to take the war out of Virginia and put the Union army in a vulnerable defensive position. General Lee's soldiers fought the Union's

Crowd at Gettysburg, November 19, 1863. President Abraham Lincoln in center.
Courtesy of the National Archives, NARA File # 111-B-4975

Army of the Potomac under the command of General George C. Meade. When the fighting ended on July 3, the two sides suffered more than 45,000 casualties, making it one of the bloodiest battles to date. Confederate forces retreated back to Virginia on the night of July 4, 1863, and the Battle of Gettysburg is considered by most scholars to be the turning point in the American Civil War.

Gettysburg Address

Four score and seven years ago our fathers brought forth on this continent, a new nation, conceived in Liberty, and dedicated to the proposition that all men are created equal.

Now we are engaged in a great civil war, testing whether that nation, or any nation so conceived and so dedicated, can long endure. We are met on a great battle-field of that war. We have come to dedicate a portion of that field, as a final resting place for those who here gave their lives that the nation might live. It is altogether fitting and proper that we should do this.

But, in a larger sense, we can not dedicate—we can not consecrate—we can not hallow—this ground. The brave men, living and dead, who struggled here, have consecrated it, far above our poor power to add or detract. The world will little note, nor long remember what we say here, but it can never forget what they did here. It is for us the living, rather, to be dedicated here to the unfinished work which they who fought here have thus far so nobly advanced. It is rather for us to be here dedicated to the great task remaining before us—that from these honored dead we take increased devotion to that cause for which they gave the last full measure of devotion—that we here highly resolve that these dead shall not have died in vain—that this nation, under God, shall have a new birth of freedom—and that government of the people, by the people, for the people, shall not perish from the earth.

The Four Freedoms (1941)
Franklin D. Roosevelt

In January 1941, as much of Europe had fallen victim to the advancing army of Nazi Germany, Franklin D. Roosevelt began his unprecedented third term as president of the United States. Great Britain was finding it increasingly difficult to hold off the aggressive German army and Roosevelt considered the Germans to be a significant threat to U.S. national security. During his annual State of the Union address on January 6, 1941, Roosevelt pledged his support for Great Britain by continuing aid and increasing production at war industries in the United States. By aiding in the war effort, Roosevelt explained that the United States would be protecting the universal freedoms and liberties to which all people are entitled, not just Americans.

In his speech, Roosevelt staunchly defended democracy around the world and stated that the United

President Franklin D. Roosevelt.
Courtesy of the Library of Congress, LC-USZ62-117121

States would not be "intimidated by the threats of dictators." He concluded by eloquently describing "four essential human freedoms" that the United States hoped to secure and extend to all individuals. These universal freedoms were: freedom of speech and expression, freedom of every person to worship God in his own way, freedom from want, and freedom from fear.

President Franklin D. Roosevelt delivering his State of the Union address before a joint session of Congress, January 6, 1941.

Courtesy of the Library of Congress, LC-USZ62-78575

In 1943, following America's entry into World War II, artist Norman Rockwell captured the idea of these four basic freedoms in a series of paintings published in the popular magazine, The Saturday Evening Post. The paintings served as the centerpiece of an exhibition that toured the United States to help raise money for the war effort.

EXCERPTS

I address you, the Members of the Seventy-seventh Congress, at a moment unprecedented in the history of the Union. I use the word "unprecedented," because at no previous time has American security been as seriously threatened from without as it is today....

As a nation, we may take pride in the fact that we are softhearted; but we cannot afford to be soft-headed....

Just as our national policy in internal affairs has been based upon a decent respect for the rights and the dignity of all our fellow men within our gates, so our national policy in foreign affairs has been based on a decent respect for the rights and dignity of all nations, large and small. And the justice of morality must and will win in the end....

In the future days, which we seek to make secure, we look forward to a world founded upon four essential human freedoms.

The first is freedom of speech and expression—everywhere in the world.

The second is freedom of every person to worship God in his own way—everywhere in the world.

The third is freedom from want—which, translated into world terms, means economic understandings which will secure to every nation a healthy peacetime life for its inhabitants—everywhere in the world.

The fourth is freedom from fear—which, translated into world terms, means a world-wide reduction of armaments to such a point and in such a thorough fashion that no nation will be in a position to commit an act of physical aggression against any neighbor—anywhere in the world.

That is no vision of a distant millennium. It is a definite basis for a kind of world attainable in our own time and generation. That kind of world is the very antithesis of the so-called new order of tyranny which the dictators seek to create with the crash of a bomb.

To that new order we oppose the greater conception—the moral order. A good society is able to face schemes of world domination and foreign revolutions alike without fear.

Since the beginning of our American history, we have been engaged in change—in a perpetual peaceful revolution—a revolution which goes on steadily, quietly adjusting itself to changing conditions—without the concentration camp or the quick-lime in the ditch. The world order which we seek is the cooperation of free countries, working together in a friendly, civilized society.

This nation has placed its destiny in the hands and heads and hearts of its millions of free men and women; and its faith in freedom under the guidance of God. Freedom means the supremacy of human rights everywhere. Our support goes to those who struggle to gain those rights or keep them. Our strength is our unity of purpose. To that high concept there can be no end save victory.

Inaugural Address
John F. Kennedy (1961)

In 1960, John F. Kennedy defeated Richard M. Nixon to become the 35th president of the United States. A World War II hero and former representative and senator from Massachusetts, Kennedy and his young family brought an optimistic, youthful spirit to the White House. At the time, America's Cold War struggle with the Communist-led Union of Soviet Socialist Republics was becoming increasingly volatile around the world. From Germany to Cuba to Southeast Asia, tension between U.S.-supported forces and Soviet-supported forces threatened to unleash a devastating nuclear exchange.

President John F. Kennedy delivering his inaugural address, January 20, 1961.
Courtesy of the John F. Kennedy Presidential Library and Museum

On January 20, 1961, Kennedy delivered his inaugural address on the steps of the U.S. Capitol in Washington, DC. His remarks focused on the critical foreign policy issues of the time. In stating that the United States would "pay any price, bear any burden," he was signaling American resolve to support the forces of freedom in the face of the Communist challenge. Kennedy, however, also presented an alternate vision, calling on the Soviets and Americans to pursue arms control, negotiations, and the "struggle against the common enemies of man: tyranny, poverty, disease and war itself."

President John F. Kennedy.
Courtesy of the John F. Kennedy Presidential Library and Museum

As a young president, Kennedy saw himself as part of a "new generation of Americans," and he was not afraid to ask his generation to work toward a better world. In the most famous part of the speech, Kennedy challenged Americans to move beyond self-interest and work for their country, saying "Ask not what your country can do for you—ask what you can do for your country."

EXCERPTS

We observe today not a victory of party but a celebration of freedom—symbolizing an end as well as a beginning—signifying renewal as well as change. For I have sworn before you and Almighty God the same solemn oath our forbears prescribed nearly a century and three-quarters ago.

The world is very different now. For man holds in his mortal hands the power to abolish all forms of human poverty and all forms of human life. And yet the same revolutionary beliefs for which our forbears fought are still at issue around the globe—the belief that the rights of man come not from the generosity of the state but from the hand of God.

We dare not forget today that we are the heirs of that first revolution. Let the word go forth from this time and place, to friend and foe alike, that the torch has been passed to a new generation of Americans—born in this century, tempered by war, disciplined by a hard and bitter peace, proud of our ancient heritage—and unwilling to witness or permit the slow undoing of those human rights to which this nation has always been committed, and to which we are committed today at home and around the world.

Let every nation know, whether it wishes us well or ill, that we shall pay any price, bear any burden, meet any hardship, support any friend, oppose any foe to assure the survival and the success of liberty....

In the long history of the world, only a few generations have been granted the role of defending freedom in its hour of maximum danger. I do not shrink from this responsibility—I welcome it. I do not believe that any of us would exchange places with any other people or any other generation. The energy, the faith, the devotion which we bring to this endeavor will light our country and all who serve it—and the glow from that fire can truly light the world.

And so, my fellow Americans: ask not what your country can do for you—ask what you can do for your country.

My fellow citizens of the world: ask not what America will do for you, but what together we can do for the freedom of man.

Finally, whether you are citizens of America or citizens of the world, ask of us here the same high standards of strength and sacrifice which we ask of you. With a good conscience our only sure reward, with history the final judge of our deeds, let us go forth to lead the land we love, asking His blessing and His help, but knowing that here on earth God's work must truly be our own.

I Have a Dream (1963)
Martin Luther King, Jr.

On August 28, 1963, nearly 250,000 people gathered in Washington, DC, as part of the March on Washington for Jobs and Freedom. The demonstrators marched from the Washington Monument to the Lincoln Memorial where individuals from all segments of society called for civil rights and equal protection for all citizens, regardless of color or background.

The last speaker of the day was Dr. Martin Luther King, Jr., whose "I Have a Dream" speech encompassed the ideals set forth in the Declaration of Independence "that all men are created equal." King's message of freedom and democracy for all people, of all races and backgrounds, is remembered as the landmark statement of the civil rights movement in the United States.

Demonstrators at the March on Washington for Jobs and Freedom in Washington, DC, August 28, 1963. Courtesy of the Library of Congress, LC-DIG-ppmsca-03128

The following year, Congress passed the Civil Rights Act of 1964, which prohibited segregation in public places, provided for the integration of public schools and facilities, and made employment on the basis of race or ethnicity illegal. This act was the most comprehensive civil rights legislation since the reconstruction era following the American Civil War.

Excerpts

...I say to you today, my friends, so even though we face the difficulties of today and tomorrow, I still have a dream. It is a dream deeply rooted in the American dream.

I have a dream that one day this nation will rise up and live out the true meaning of its creed: "We hold these truths to be self-evident, that all men are created equal."...

I have a dream that my four little children will one day live in a nation where they will not be judged by the color of their skin but by the content of their character....

This will be the day, this will be the day when all of God's children will be able to sing with new meaning: "My country, 'tis of thee, sweet land of liberty, of thee I sing. Land where my fathers died, land of the pilgrim's pride, From every mountainside, let freedom ring!"...

And when this happens, when we allow freedom ring, when we let it ring from every village and every hamlet, from every state and every city, we will be able to speed up that day when all of God's children, black men and white men, Jews and Gentiles, Protestants and Catholics, will be able to join hands and sing in the words of the old Negro spiritual: "Free at last! Free at last! Thank God Almighty, we are free at last!"

Remarks at the (1987) Brandenburg Gate

Ronald Reagan

On June 12, 1987, President Ronald Reagan delivered a formal address to the people of West Berlin in front of the Brandenburg Gate, a once proud symbol of German unity. At the time, a wall surrounding West Berlin separated the city from East Berlin and other areas of East Germany. The barrier, known as the Berlin Wall, was heavily guarded and East Germany's Communist government did not allow its people access to West Berlin. The Berlin Wall was a symbol of the tyranny that restrained freedom and individual liberty throughout the Communist bloc of Eastern Europe.

Because of the gate's proximity to East Berlin, Reagan's speech could be heard on the Eastern side of the wall as well. In his remarks, he spoke of the increasing divide

President Ronald Reagan delivering his address at the Brandenburg Gate in West Berlin, June 12, 1987.
Courtesy of the Ronald Reagan Presidential Library

between the freedom and prosperity of the West and the political slavery of Communist Eastern Europe, dominated at the time by the Union of Soviet Socialist Republics. Reagan imagined a world in which East and West were united in freedom rather than oppression. He believed that ultimately totalitarianism and oppression could not suppress the freedoms that are entitled to all individuals. Reagan's direct challenge to Soviet leader Mikhail Gorbachev, saying "If you seek peace, if you seek prosperity for the Soviet Union and Eastern Europe, if you seek liberalization…Mr. Gorbachev, tear down this wall!" is considered by many to have affirmed the dissolution of the Soviet Union and the end of the Communist stronghold over Eastern Europe.

EXCERPTS

…Behind me stands a wall that encircles the free sectors of this city, part of a vast system of barriers that divides the entire continent of Europe. From the Baltic, south, those barriers cut across Germany in a gash of barbed wire, concrete, dog runs, and guard towers. Farther south, there may be no visible, no obvious wall. But there remain armed guards and checkpoints all the same—still a restriction on the right to travel, still an instrument to impose upon ordinary men and women the will of a totalitarian state. Yet it is here in Berlin where the wall emerges most clearly; here, cutting across your city, where the news photo and the television screen have imprinted this brutal division of a continent upon the mind of the world. Standing before the Brandenburg Gate, every man is a German, separated from his fellow men. Every man is a Berliner, forced to look upon a scar.…

General Secretary Gorbachev, if you seek peace, if you seek prosperity for the Soviet Union and Eastern Europe, if you seek liberalization: Come here to this gate! Mr. Gorbachev, open this gate! Mr. Gorbachev, tear down this wall!

Fundamental Documents of American Democracy

In its most basic form, the U.S. system of government is a mutual agreement between the people and the government to ensure that individual liberties are maintained and continue to prosper under a free society. This idea was established upon the signing of the Mayflower Compact by some of America's first settlers, the Pilgrims, in 1620. The Declaration of Independence, signed on July 4, 1776, listed America's reasons for independence from Great Britain, but also further explained the rights of free people and how they should live under a responsible government.

As it developed into a nation, based upon the firm foundation of the Constitution, the United States government has continued to adapt in order to live up to its promise of liberty and equality for all individuals. The *Federalist Papers*, written between 1787 and 1788, give today's citizens a remarkable look into the framing of our government more than 200 years ago. Through the Bill of Rights and seventeen subsequent amendments, the Constitution has been changed over the years to solidify America's promise of liberty for all its citizens. The following section introduces you to these, and other important documents, that have helped make the United States the land of opportunity it is today.

The Mayflower Compact (1620)

In the late 1500s, several religious groups in England wanted to establish a new church completely independent from the Church of England. These individuals were called "separatists" and were often persecuted because of their religious practices and beliefs. One of these groups became known as the Pilgrims. After continuously being denied the right to establish their own church in England, the Pilgrims decided to move their families to Holland. While Holland allowed them to worship freely, the Pilgrims soon began to miss the language and customs of life in England. After much discussion, the Pilgrims decided to move the entire community to America, where they could practice their religious beliefs and still maintain an English lifestyle.

On September 6, 1620, their ship, called the "Mayflower," set sail for America. Two months later, the Pilgrims landed off the coast of Massachusetts, much further north than they originally intended. Since this land was outside the

Signing the Mayflower Compact. Courtesy of the Library of Congress, LC-USZ61-206

jurisdiction of the Virginia Colony's government in Jamestown, the group agreed to draft a social contract for self-government based on consent of the governed and majority rule. All male adults signed the contract and agreed to be bound by its rules. This agreement became known as the Mayflower Compact and was the first act of European self-government in America. The concept that government is a form of covenant between two parties, the government and the people, was a major source of inspiration to the framers of the U.S. Constitution.

THE MAYFLOWER COMPACT

We whose names are underwritten, the loyal subjects of our dread Sovereign Lord King James, by the Grace of God of Great Britain, France and Ireland, King, Defender of the Faith, etc.

Having undertaken, for the Glory of God and advancement of the Christian Faith and Honour of our King and Country, a Voyage to plant the First Colony in the Northern Parts of Virginia, do by these presents solemnly and mutually in the presence of God and one of another, Covenant and Combine ourselves together into a Civil Body Politic, for our better ordering and preservation and furtherance of the ends aforesaid; and by virtue hereof to enact, constitute and frame such just and equal Laws, Ordinances, Acts, Constitutions and Offices, from time to time, as shall be thought most meet and convenient for the general good of the Colony, unto which we promise all due submission and obedience. In witness whereof we have hereunder subscribed our names at Cape Cod, the 11th of November, in the year of the reign of our Sovereign Lord King James, of England, France and Ireland the eighteenth, and of Scotland the fifty-fourth. Anno Domini 1620.

The Declaration of Independence (1776)

Following the end of the French and Indian War in 1763, Great Britain established itself as the dominant power in North America. The victory greatly increased the British presence in North America, but left the British government with a significant amount of debt. Frustrated by what was perceived as a lack of cooperation during the French and Indian War, Great Britain demanded that, at the very least, the colonists should pay for the cost of their own government and security.

The British began tightening control over the colonies by bypassing colonial legislatures and imposing direct taxes and laws that angered many American colonists. In 1764, the Sugar Act was enacted by the British Parliament and became the first law with the specific goal of raising money from the colonies. This law was followed by the Currency Act which prohibited the colonies from issuing their own currency, the Quartering Act, which required the colonies to provide housing and supplies for British troops, and the Stamp

The Destruction of Tea at Boston Harbor, 1773. Courtesy of the National Archives, NARA File # 148-GW-439

Act, which directly taxed the colonies by requiring all documents and packages to obtain a stamp showing that the tax had been paid. Violations of these acts often led to harsh judgments by British-appointed judges without the consent of local juries.

American colonists responded to these acts with organized protest, arguing against taxation without proper representation in Parliament. They believed that the strong measures enacted by the government violated their rights as British citizens. The colonists also believed that government should not interfere in the daily lives of its citizens, but should serve to secure and protect the liberty and property of the people.

On September 5, 1774, delegates from twelve of the thirteen colonies convened in Philadelphia, Pennsylvania, for the First Continental Congress. During the meeting, they prepared a petition, called the Declaration of Rights and Grievances, for King George III, king of the United Kingdom of Great Britain and Ireland. They also established the Association of 1774, which urged the colonists to avoid using British goods. Before adjourning, the delegates planned for a Second Continental Congress to meet on May 10, 1775,

The committee of Congress drafting the Declaration of Independence, 1776.
Courtesy of the Library of Congress, LC-USZ62-17878

in case the British failed to respond adequately to its petition.

The Second Continental Congress convened in May 1775 and following much debate, agreed that reconciliation with Britain was impossible. On June 7, 1776, Virginia delegate Richard Henry Lee called for a resolution of independence. Congress then appointed John Adams, Benjamin Franklin, Thomas Jefferson, Robert R. Livingston, and Roger Sherman to draft a statement of independence for the colonies, with Jefferson assigned to perform the actual writing of the document.

In writing the Declaration of Independence, Jefferson drew heavily upon the idea of natural rights and individual liberty. These

In "*Declaration of Independence*," a painting by John Trumbull, Thomas Jefferson and his committee present the formal statement of independence from Great Britain.

ideas had been widely expressed by 17th century philosopher John Locke, and others, at that time. The beginning of the document explains that "All men are created equal, that they are endowed by their Creator with certain unalienable Rights, that among these are Life, Liberty and the pursuit of Happiness." Jefferson then listed formal grievances against Great Britain, thus justifying the colonies' decision to completely break away from the mother country. On July 2, 1776, the document was sent to Congress for consideration and debate. Two days later, on July 4, 1776, Congress unanimously adopted the Declaration of Independence.

Of the fifty-six signers of the Declaration of Independence, eight were foreign-born. They included: Button Gwinnett (England), Francis Lewis (Wales), Robert Morris (England), James Smith (Ireland), George Taylor (Ireland), Matthew Thornton (Ireland), James Wilson (Scotland), and John Witherspoon (Scotland).

THE DECLARATION OF INDEPENDENCE

Action of Second Continental Congress, July 4, 1776
The Unanimous Declaration of the thirteen united States of America

WHEN in the Course of human Events, it becomes necessary for one People to dissolve the Political Bands which have connected them with another, and to assume among the Powers of the Earth, the separate and equal Station to which the Laws of Nature and of Nature's God entitle them, a decent Respect to the Opinions of Mankind requires that they should declare the causes which impel them to the Separation.

WE hold these Truths to be self-evident, that all Men are created equal, that they are endowed by their Creator with certain unalienable Rights, that among these are Life, Liberty, and the pursuit of Happiness—That to secure these Rights, Governments are instituted among Men, deriving their just Powers from the Consent of the Governed, that whenever any Form of Government becomes destructive of these Ends, it is the Right of the People to alter or to abolish it, and to institute new Government, laying its Foundation on such Principles, and organizing its Powers in such Form, as to them shall seem most likely to effect their Safety and Happiness. Prudence, indeed, will dictate that Governments long established should not be changed for light and transient Causes; and accordingly all Experience hath shewn, that Mankind are more disposed to suffer, while Evils are sufferable, than to right themselves by abolishing the Forms to which they are accustomed. But when a long Train of Abuses and Usurpations, pursuing invariably the same Object, evinces a design to reduce them under absolute Despotism, it is their Right, it is their Duty, to throw off such Government, and to provide new Guards for their future Security. Such has been the patient Sufferance of these Colonies; and such is now the Necessity which constrains them to alter their former Systems of Government. The History of the present King of Great-Britain is a History of repeated Injuries and Usurpations, all having in direct Object the Establishment of an absolute Tyranny over these States. To prove this, let Facts be submitted to a candid World.

HE has refused his Assent to Laws, the most wholesome and necessary for the public Good.

HE has forbidden his Governors to pass Laws of immediate and pressing Importance, unless suspended in their Operation till his Assent should be obtained; and when so suspended, he has utterly neglected to attend to them.

HE has refused to pass other Laws for the Accommodation of large Districts of People, unless those People would relinquish the Right of Representation in the Legislature, a Right inestimable to them, and formidable to Tyrants only.

HE has called together Legislative Bodies at Places unusual, uncomfortable, and distant from the Depository of their public Records, for the sole Purpose of fatiguing them into Compliance with his Measures.

HE has dissolved Representative Houses repeatedly, for opposing with manly Firmness his Invasions on the Rights of the People.

HE has refused for a long Time, after such Dissolutions, to cause others to be elected; whereby the Legislative Powers, incapable of Annihilation, have returned to the People at large for their exercise; the State remaining in the mean time exposed to all the Dangers of Invasion from without, and Convulsions within.

HE has endeavoured to prevent the Population of these States; for that Purpose obstructing the Laws for Naturalization of Foreigners; refusing to pass others to encourage their Migrations hither, and raising the Conditions of new Appropriations of Lands.

HE has obstructed the Administration of Justice, by refusing his Assent to Laws for establishing Judiciary Powers.

HE has made Judges dependent on his Will alone, for the Tenure of their Offices, and the Amount and Payment of their Salaries.

HE has erected a Multitude of new Offices, and sent hither Swarms of Officers to harrass our People, and eat out their Substance.

HE has kept among us, in Times of Peace, Standing Armies, without the consent of our Legislatures.

HE has affected to render the Military independent of and superior to the Civil Power.

HE has combined with others to subject us to a Jurisdiction foreign to our Constitution, and unacknowledged by our Laws; giving his Assent to their Acts of pretended Legislation:

FOR quartering large Bodies of Armed Troops among us:

FOR protecting them, by a mock Trial, from Punishment for any Murders which they should commit on the Inhabitants of these States:

FOR cutting off our Trade with all Parts of the World:

FOR imposing Taxes on us without our Consent:

FOR depriving us, in many Cases, of the Benefits of Trial by Jury:

FOR transporting us beyond Seas to be tried for pretended Offences:

FOR abolishing the free System of English Laws in a neighbouring Province, establishing therein an arbitrary Government, and enlarging its Boundaries, so as to render it at once an Example and fit Instrument for introducing the same absolute Rule into these Colonies:

FOR taking away our Charters, abolishing our most valuable Laws, and altering fundamentally the Forms of our Governments:

FOR suspending our own Legislatures, and declaring themselves invested with Power to legislate for us in all Cases whatsoever.

HE has abdicated Government here, by declaring us out of his Protection and waging War against us.

HE has plundered our Seas, ravaged our Coasts, burnt our Towns, and destroyed the Lives of our People.

HE is, at this Time, transporting large Armies of foreign Mercenaries to compleat the Works of Death, Desolation, and Tyranny, already begun with circumstances of Cruelty and Perfidy, scarcely paralleled in the most barbarous Ages, and totally unworthy the Head of a civilized Nation.

HE has constrained our fellow Citizens taken Captive on the high Seas to bear Arms against their Country, to become the Executioners of their Friends and Brethren, or to fall themselves by their Hands.

HE has excited domestic Insurrections amongst us, and has endeavoured to bring on the Inhabitants of our Frontiers, the merciless Indian Savages, whose known Rule of Warfare, is an undistinguished Destruction of all Ages, Sexes and Conditions.

IN every stage of these Oppressions we have Petitioned for Redress in the most humble Terms: Our repeated Petitions have been answered only by repeated Injury. A Prince, whose Character is thus marked by every act which may define a Tyrant, is unfit to be the Ruler of a free People.

NOR have we been wanting in Attentions to our British Brethren. We have warned them from Time to Time of Attempts by their Legislature to extend an unwarrantable Jurisdiction over us. We have reminded them of the Circumstances of our Emigration and Settlement here. We have appealed to their native Justice and Magnanimity, and we have conjured them by the Ties of our common Kindred to disavow these Usurpations, which, would inevitably interrupt our Connections and Correspondence. They too have been deaf to the Voice of Justice and of Consanguinity. We must, therefore, acquiesce in the Necessity, which denounces our Separation, and hold them, as we hold the rest of Mankind, Enemies in War, in Peace, Friends.

We, therefore, the Representatives of the united States of America, in General Congress, Assembled, appealing to the Supreme Judge of the World for the Rectitude of our Intentions, do, in the Name, and by Authority of the good People of these Colonies, solemnly Publish and Declare, That these United Colonies are, and of Right ought to be Free and Independent States; that they are absolved from all Allegiance to the British Crown, and that all political Connection between them and the State of Great-Britain, is and ought to be totally dissolved; and that as Free and Independent States, they have full Power to levy War, conclude Peace, contract Alliances, establish Commerce, and to do all other Acts and Things which Independent States may of right do. —And for the support of this Declaration, with a firm Reliance on the Protection of divine Providence, we mutually pledge to each other our Lives, our Fortunes, and our sacred Honor.

Signed by ORDER and in BEHALF of the CONGRESS,

JOHN HANCOCK, President

Attest.

CHARLES THOMSON, Secretary

SIGNERS OF THE DECLARATION OF INDEPENDENCE

Georgia:
Button Gwinnett
Lyman Hall
George Walton

North Carolina:
William Hooper
Joseph Hewes
John Penn

South Carolina:
Edward Rutledge
Thomas Heyward, Jr.
Thomas Lynch, Jr.
Arthur Middleton

Massachusetts:
Samuel Adams
John Adams
Robert Treat Paine
Elbridge Gerry
John Hancock

Maryland:
Samuel Chase
William Paca
Thomas Stone
Charles Carroll of
    Carrollton

Virginia:
George Wythe
Richard Henry Lee
Thomas Jefferson
Benjamin Harrison
Thomas Nelson, Jr.
Francis Lightfoot Lee
Carter Braxton

Pennsylvania:
Robert Morris
Benjamin Rush
Benjamin Franklin
John Morton
George Clymer

James Smith
George Taylor
James Wilson
George Ross

Delaware:
Caesar Rodney
George Read
Thomas McKean

New York:
William Floyd
Philip Livingston
Francis Lewis
Lewis Morris

New Jersey:
Richard Stockton
John Witherspoon
Francis Hopkinson
John Hart
Abraham Clark

New Hampshire:
Josiah Bartlett
Matthew Thornton
William Whipple

Rhode Island:
Stephen Hopkins
William Ellery

Connecticut:
Roger Sherman
Samuel Huntington
William Williams
Oliver Wolcott

The Federalist Papers (1787-1788) by Alexander Hamilton, John Jay, and James Madison

Following the Constitutional Convention in 1787, a national debate began concerning whether or not to ratify the proposed United States Constitution. Newspapers across the Nation published essays and letters on both sides—for and against ratification. The most famous of these writings became known as the *Federalist Papers*.

The *Federalist Papers* were a series of eighty-five essays written by Alexander Hamilton, John Jay, and James Madison under the pen name "Publius." The essays were published primarily in the *Independent Journal* and the *New York Packet* and their purpose was to urge New York delegates to ratify the proposed United States Constitution. In 1788, the essays were published in a bound volume.

The essays explain particular provisions of the United States Constitution in specific detail.

Title Page of The Federalist, vol. 1, 1799.
Courtesy of the Library of Congress, LC-USZ62-70508

Alexander Hamilton and James Madison were both members of the Constitutional Convention and for this reason the *Federalist Papers* offer an exciting look into the intentions of those drafting the United States Constitution. Today, the *Federalist Papers* are considered to be one of the most important historical documents on the founding principles of the United States' form of government.

No. 2 (John Jay)

To all general purposes we have uniformly been one people; each individual citizen everywhere enjoying the same national rights, privileges, and protection.

John Jay.
Courtesy of the Library of Congress, LC-USZ62-50375

No. 22 (Alexander Hamilton)

The fabric of American empire ought to rest on the solid basis of the consent of the people. The streams of national power ought to flow from that pure, original fountain of all legitimate authority.

Alexander Hamilton.
Courtesy of the Library of Congress, LC-USZC4-6423

No. 41 (James Madison)

Every man who loves peace, every man who loves his country, every man who loves liberty, ought to have it ever before his eyes, that he may cherish in his heart a due attachment to the Union of America, and be able to set a due value on the means of preserving it.

James Madison.
Courtesy of the Library of Congress, LC-USZ62-87924

No. 46 (James Madison)

[T]he ultimate authority...resides in the people alone.

No. 51 (Alexander Hamilton or James Madison)

But what is government itself, but the greatest of all reflections on human nature? If men were angels, no government would be necessary. If angels were to govern men, neither external nor internal controls on government would be necessary.

The Constitution (1787) of the United States

I n May 1787, fifty-five delegates from each of the thirteen states, with the exception of Rhode Island, convened in Philadelphia, Pennsylvania, to revise the Articles of Confederation and create a more centralized form of government for the United States. Two competing plans were presented to the delegates— Edmund Randolph's Virginia Plan and William Patterson's New Jersey Plan. The Virginia Plan would create a more powerful central government with three components: an executive, legislative, and judiciary sharing power. The New Jersey Plan would revise and amend the current Articles of Confederation to give Congress control over taxes and trade, but still provide each of the states with basic autonomy at the local level.

Through extensive debate, it soon became clear that amending the

In "Scene at the Signing of the Constitution," artist Howard Chandler Christy depicts Independence Hall in Philadelphia, PA, on September 17, 1787. Courtesy of the Library of Congress, LC-USA7-34630

Articles of Confederation would not be sufficient and a new form of government would need to be established. The most contentious issues included how much power the central government would have, how the states would be represented in Congress, and how these representatives would be elected. The final document, which was signed on September 17, 1787, combined ideas from both the Virginia and New Jersey Plans, creating a central government with three branches and giving states equal representation in the Senate regardless of state size.

Representation in the lower chamber, the House of Representatives, was based on state population.

The Constitution of the United States is the "supreme law of the land" and serves as the basic legal framework for the U.S. system of government. It has lasted longer than any other nation's constitution. It has been revised, or amended, only twenty-seven times since 1787. James Madison, a Virginia delegate and fourth president of the United States, is known as the "Father of the Constitution."

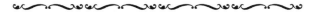

The Preamble to the Constitution

We the People of the United States, in Order to form a more perfect Union, establish Justice, insure domestic Tranquility, provide for the common defence, promote the general Welfare, and secure the Blessings of Liberty to ourselves and our Posterity, do ordain and establish this Constitution for the United States of America.

★ For the complete text of the Constitution of the United States and its subsequent amendments, including the Bill of Rights, see Form M-654.

The Bill of Rights (1791)

Following the successful creation of a new Constitution, which outlined the form and structure of the U.S. government, a public debate concerning the need to protect individual freedoms arose. Many believed that guarantees of individual rights were not needed because, under the Constitution, the people held all power not specifically granted to the central government. Others, with the memory of British tyranny fresh in their minds, demanded a list of individual rights that would be guaranteed to all citizens.

As the debate wore on, Thomas Jefferson, then serving as ambassador to France, wrote a letter to James Madison back in America stating, "A bill of rights is what the people are entitled to against every government on earth, general or particular, and what no just government should refuse, or rest on inference." This position quickly gained popularity and a compromise was finally reached. Several states, in their formal ratification of the Constitution, asked for such amendments, while others ratified the Constitution with

Copy of the twelve amendments to the Constitution as passed by Congress on September 25, 1789.
Courtesy of the Library of Congress, rbpe 00000600

the understanding that the amendments would be offered during the first meeting of Congress.

On September 25, 1789, the First Congress of the United States offered twelve amendments to the Constitution that addressed individual freedoms. Two were not ratified immediately, but the remaining ten were ratified by three-fourths of the state legislatures on December 15, 1791. These first ten amendments became known as the Bill of Rights.

Emancipation Proclamation
Abraham Lincoln (1863)

As the fierce fighting of the American Civil War entered its third year, President Abraham Lincoln acted to give a new war aim to the soldiers of the Union army. On January 1, 1863, Lincoln signed the Emancipation Proclamation, which effectively freed the slaves in the states openly rebelling against the United States. The Civil War quickly became not only a fight to preserve the Union, but also a cause for the spread of freedom to all Americans. Many of the recently freed slaves joined the Union army or navy, and fought bravely for the freedom of others.

The proclamation was greeted with celebration in Boston, New York, Washington, DC, and elsewhere. In order for these words to become reality, however, much more fighting was still to come. By the end of the American Civil War in 1865, almost 200,000 African Americans had fought for the Union. In December of that year, the U.S. Constitution was amended to free all slaves living in any part of the United States. The Thirteenth Amendment completed the work that the Emancipation Proclamation had begun—ending all slavery in the United States.

"First Reading of the Emancipation Proclamation of President Lincoln" by Francis Bicknell Carpenter.

Courtesy of the U.S. Senate, Catalog# 33.00005.000

~~~~~~

EMANCIPATION PROCLAMATION

January 1, 1863

By the President of the United States of America:

A Proclamation.

Whereas, on the twenty-second day of September, in the year of our Lord one thousand eight hundred and sixty-two, a proclamation was issued by the President of the United States, containing, among other things, the following, to wit:

"That on the first day of January, in the year of our Lord one thousand eight hundred and sixty-three, all persons held as slaves within any State or designated part of a State, the people whereof shall then be in rebellion against the United States, shall be then, thenceforward, and forever free; and the Executive Government of the United States, including the military and naval authority thereof, will recognize and maintain the freedom of such persons, and will do no act or acts to repress such persons, or any of them, in any efforts they may make for their actual freedom.

"That the Executive will, on the first day of January aforesaid, by proclamation, designate the States and parts of States, if any, in which the people thereof, respectively, shall then be in rebellion against the United States; and the fact that any State, or the people thereof, shall on that day be, in good faith, represented in the Congress of the United States by members chosen thereto at elections wherein a majority of the qualified voters of such State shall have participated, shall, in the absence of strong countervailing testimony, be deemed conclusive evidence that such State, and the people thereof, are not then in rebellion against the United States."

Now, therefore I, Abraham Lincoln, President of the United States, by virtue of the power in me vested as Commander-in-Chief, of the Army and Navy of the United States in time of actual armed rebellion against the authority and government of the United States, and as a fit and necessary war measure for suppressing said rebellion, do, on this first day of January, in the year of our Lord one thousand eight hundred and sixty-three, and in accordance with my purpose so to do publicly proclaimed for the full period of one hundred days, from the day first above mentioned, order and designate as the States and parts of States wherein the people thereof respectively, are this day in rebellion against the United States, the following, to wit:

Arkansas, Texas, Louisiana, (except the Parishes of St. Bernard, Plaquemines, Jefferson, St. John, St. Charles, St. James Ascension, Assumption, Terrebonne, Lafourche, St. Mary, St. Martin, and Orleans, including the City of New Orleans) Mississippi, Alabama, Florida, Georgia, South Carolina, North Carolina, and Virginia, (except the forty-eight counties designated as West Virginia, and also the counties of Berkley, Accomac, Northampton, Elizabeth City, York, Princess Ann, and Norfolk, including the cities of Norfolk and Portsmouth[)], and which excepted parts, are for the present, left precisely as if this proclamation were not issued.

And by virtue of the power, and for the purpose aforesaid, I do order and declare that all persons held as slaves within said designated States, and parts of States, are, and henceforward shall be free; and that the Executive government of the United States, including the military and naval authorities thereof, will recognize and maintain the freedom of said persons.

And I hereby enjoin upon the people so declared to be free to abstain from all violence, unless in necessary self-defence; and I recommend to them that, in all cases when allowed, they labor faithfully for reasonable wages.

And I further declare and make known, that such persons of suitable condition, will be received into the armed service of the United States to garrison forts, positions, stations, and other places, and to man vessels of all sorts in said service.

And upon this act, sincerely believed to be an act of justice, warranted by the Constitution, upon military necessity, I invoke the considerate judgment of mankind, and the gracious favor of Almighty God.

In witness whereof, I have hereunto set my hand and caused the seal of the United States to be affixed.

Done at the City of Washington, this first day of January, in the year of our Lord one thousand eight hundred and sixty three, and of the Independence of the United States of America the eighty-seventh.

By the President: ABRAHAM LINCOLN

WILLIAM H. SEWARD, Secretary of State.

President *Abraham* Lincoln on the battlefield of *Antietam*, October 1862. The Battle of *Antietam* ended the Confederate Army of Northern *Virginia's* first invasion into the North and led to President Lincoln's issuance of the preliminary Emancipation Proclamation.

Landmark Decisions of the U.S. Supreme Court

Since it first convened in 1790, the U.S. Supreme Court has been the central arena for debate on some of America's most important social and public policy issues including civil rights, powers of government, and equal opportunity. As the ultimate authority on constitutional law, the Supreme Court attempts to settle disputes when it appears that federal, state, or local laws conflict with the Constitution. The Supreme Court's decisions determine how America's principles and ideals, as expressed in the Constitution, are carried out in everyday life. These decisions impact the lives of all Americans. In the following section, you will read about several landmark decisions of the Supreme Court that are important to know and understand as a United States citizen.

Marbury v. Madison
John Marshall
Delivering the Opinion of the Court (1803)

While the U.S. Supreme Court wields immense power in determining the constitutionality of federal laws, its authority was still uncertain until 1803. Although most of the framers expected the Supreme Court to perform this essential role, the Court's authority was not explicitly defined in the Constitution. Chief Justice John Marshall's decision in *Marbury v. Madison*, speaking for a unanimous Court, established the power of judicial review, making the Supreme Court an equal partner in government along with the Legislative and Executive branches. The Supreme Court now serves as the final authority on the Constitution.

The *Marbury* case began in 1801, during the last few weeks of President John Adams's term as president, just before Thomas Jefferson assumed the presidency.

Congress had recently approved the appointment of several new justices of the peace in and around the District of Columbia. President Adams made appointments to

Chief Justice John Marshall.
Courtesy of the Library of Congress, LC-USZ62-8499

these positions, and the Senate confirmed each just one day before Jefferson took office. The secretary of state was to deliver the formal appointments prior to Jefferson taking office, however, many of the commissions were not delivered on time. One of those appointed, William Marbury, did not receive his commission and immediately filed suit against the new Secretary of State, James Madison, for failing to deliver it promptly.

Marbury went directly to the Supreme Court, seeking a writ of mandamus, a legal order demanding compliance with the law, to require Secretary Madison to deliver the commission. Chief Justice John Marshall was aware that if the Court forced Madison to deliver the commission, Jefferson and his administration would most likely ignore it, and thus undermine the authority of the Court. Marshall's decision stated that Madison should have delivered the commission to Marbury, but the section of the Judiciary Act of 1789 that gave the Supreme Court the power to issue writs of mandamus exceeded the authority of the Court under Article III of the Constitution. The decision upheld the law as defined in the Constitution, limiting the Supreme Court's power at the same time, and establishing the fundamental principle of judicial review.

EXCERPTS

...The question, whether an act, repugnant to the constitution, can become the law of the land, is a question deeply interesting to the United States;... That the people have an original right to establish, for their future government, such principles as, in their opinion, shall most conduce to their own happiness, is the basis on which the whole American fabric has been erected....

This original and supreme will organizes the government, and assigns to different departments their respective powers. It may either stop here, or establish certain limits not to be transcended by those departments.

The government of the United States is of the latter description. The powers of the legislature are defined and limited; and that those limits may not be mistaken, or forgotten, the constitution is written.... The distinction between a government with limited and unlimited powers is abolished, if those limits do not confine the persons on whom they are imposed, and if acts prohibited and acts allowed, are of equal obligation. It is a proposition too plain to be contested, that the constitution controls any legislative act repugnant to it; or, that the legislature may alter the constitution by an ordinary act. Between these alternatives there is no middle ground....

Certainly all those who have framed written constitutions contemplate them as forming the fundamental and paramount law of the nation, and consequently, the theory of every such government must be, that an act of the legislature, repugnant to the constitution, is void.

This theory is essentially attached to a written constitution, and is, consequently, to be considered, by this court, as one of the fundamental principles of our society....

Plessy v. Ferguson
John Marshall Harlan
Delivering the Dissenting (1896) Opinion of the Court

While great strides were made in establishing the political rights of African Americans following the American Civil War, the U.S. Supreme Court delivered several decisions, most notably in the case of *Plessy v. Ferguson*, that impeded civil rights efforts in the United States.

Beginning in 1887, following the passage of the first "Jim Crow" laws in Florida, states began to require that railroads furnish separate accommodations for each race. "Jim Crow" laws sought to restrict the rights of African Americans. They were named after a popular minstrel character in the 1830s. The laws were unfair, and by this time, segregation was extended to most public facilities. Many saw the extension of segregation into railroads as a further objection of the work that Congress and the

Justice John Marshall Harlan.
Courtesy of the Library of Congress, LC-BH832-1038

federal government had done to affirm the rights of African Americans.

On June 7, 1892, Homer Plessy, an African American from New Orleans, boarded a train and sat in a rail car for white passengers. A conductor asked him to move, but Plessy refused, and was then arrested and charged with violating the Jim Crow Car Act of 1890. Plessy challenged his arrest in court and the case was tried in New Orleans. He argued that segregation violated both the Thirteenth and Fourteenth Amendments to the U.S. Constitution. Through appeal, the case was heard before the U.S. Supreme Court in 1896. By an eight to one decision, the Court ruled against Plessy, thus establishing the "separate but equal" rule. The "separate but equal" rule mandated separate accommodations for blacks and whites on buses, trains, and in hotels, theaters, and schools.

In a powerful dissent, Justice John Marshall Harlan disagreed with the majority, stating "Our Constitution is color-blind, and neither knows nor tolerates classes among citizens." Harlan's words provided inspiration to many involved in the civil rights movement, including Thurgood Marshall, whose arguments in *Brown v. Board of Education* helped overturn the "separate but equal" precedent in 1954.

EXCERPTS

In respect of civil rights, common to all citizens, the Constitution of the United States does not, I think permit any public authority to know the race of those entitled to be protected in the enjoyment of such rights.... [I]n the view of the Constitution, in the eye of the law, there is in this country no superior, dominant, ruling class of citizens. There is no caste here. Our Constitution is color-blind and neither knows nor tolerates classes among citizens. In respect of civil rights, all citizens are equal before the law. The humblest is the peer of the most powerful. The law regards man as man and takes no account of his surroundings or of his color when his civil rights as guaranteed by the supreme law of the land are involved....

West Virginia State Board of Education v. Barnette (1943)

Robert Jackson Delivering the Opinion of the Court

In 1940, as most of Europe was at war with Nazi Germany and the United States was increasing production at its war industries in support of Great Britain, a wave of patriotism swept the country. During this time, the U.S. Supreme Court ruled in *Minersville School District v. Gobitis* that public school students were required to salute the American flag and recite the Pledge of Allegiance regardless of personal religious beliefs. Despite the ruling, many students, including the children of Jehovah's Witnesses, a religious group in the United States, continued to resist saluting the flag and reciting the Pledge of Allegiance due to their religious beliefs. Many of these students were persecuted for their beliefs and intense pressure forced the Supreme Court to revisit the issue of First Amendment freedoms just three years later.

In 1943, the Court heard arguments in the case of *West Virginia State Board of Education v. Barnette*. This case concerned a requirement by the West Virginia Board of Education that all teachers and students must salute the flag

A visiting rabbi teaching Orthodox religion to children in Jersey Homesteads, NJ, 1936.

Courtesy of the Library of Congress, LC-USF33-011049-M4

A church service on Thanksgiving Day, 1942.
Courtesy of the Library of Congress, LC-USE6-D-006812

as part of their daily program. Refusal to do so resulted in harsh punishment, including, in some cases, expulsion. After reviewing arguments on both sides, the Court reversed its original ruling in *Minersville School District v. Gobitis*, stating that this required activity violated the First Amendment. Justice Robert Jackson delivered the decision of the majority, writing that "If there is any fixed star in our constitutional constellation, it is that no official, high or petty, can prescribe what shall be orthodox in politics, nationalism, religion, or other matters of opinion or force citizens to confess by word or act their faith therein." The Court's ruling ensured that the right to worship freely, as long as it does not interfere with the rights of others, is protected under the Constitution.

EXCERPTS

...The very purpose of a Bill of Rights was to withdraw certain subjects from the vicissitudes of political controversy, to place them beyond the reach of majorities and officials and to establish them as legal principles to be applied by the courts. One's right to life, liberty, and property, to free speech, a free press, freedom of worship and assembly, and other fundamental rights may not be submitted to vote; they depend on the outcome of no elections....

If there is any fixed star in our constitutional constellation, it is that no official, high or petty, can prescribe what shall be orthodox in politics, nationalism, religion, or other matters of opinion or force citizens to confess by word or act their faith therein. If there are any circumstances which permit an exception, they do not now occur to us....

Brown v. Board of Education (1954)
Earl Warren Delivering the Opinion of the Court

Since the U.S. Supreme Court's 1896 decision in the case of *Plessy v. Ferguson*, racially segregated public schools were accepted under the basis of the "separate but equal" rule. The "separate but equal" rule mandated separate accommodations for blacks and whites on buses, trains, and in hotels, theaters, and schools. Many civil rights groups, including the National Association for the Advancement of Colored People (NAACP), worked to overturn this ruling for several decades. In 1952, the NAACP brought five cases before the Supreme Court that directly challenged the precedent established in *Plessy v. Ferguson*. Due to the

Integrated classroom at Anacostia High School, Washington, DC, 1957.
Courtesy of the Library of Congress, LC-U9-1033-16

divided opinion of the Court on whether or not it was possible to overturn this ruling, the justices called for additional hearings at a later date.

Following several setbacks, including the death of Chief Justice Frederick Vinson, the Supreme Court agreed to hear each case once again during its 1953 term. The five cases brought before the Supreme Court illustrated that many public schools in America were not providing equal facilities and materials to African American students. Thurgood Marshall, the NAACP's lead attorney, argued that the "separate but equal" rule violated the Fourteenth Amendment to the Constitution, which granted citizenship to all citizens regardless of color, and provided equal protection under the law.

On May 17, 1954, Chief Justice Earl Warren delivered the unanimous ruling of the Court, stating that the segregation of public schools was in fact a violation of the Fourteenth Amendment and was therefore unconstitutional. This historic decision ended the "separate but equal" rule that had been in place for nearly six decades. The Court's opinion in this landmark case helped expand the civil rights movement in the United States, advancing the idea that every citizen deserves America's promise of equality and justice under the law.

Excerpts

...We come then to the question presented: Does segregation of children in public schools solely on the basis of race, even though the physical facilities and other "tangible" factors may be equal, deprive the children of the minority group of equal educational opportunities? We believe that it does.... To separate them from others of similar age and qualifications solely because of their race generates a feeling of inferiority as to their status in the community that may affect their heart and minds in a way unlikely ever to be undone....

We conclude that in the field of public education the doctrine of "separate but equal" has no place. Separate educational facilities are inherently unequal....

Presidential Statements on Citizenship and Immigration

The United States has a long, cherished history as a welcoming country and the contributions of immigrants continue to enrich the nation. While our citizens come from different backgrounds and cultures, Americans are bound together by shared ideals, based on individual freedom and the rule of law. American presidents, beginning with George Washington, have acknowledged the contributions of immigrants and regularly spoken about the importance of responsible citizenship.

Speaking on behalf of the United States and its citizens, presidential speeches are often eloquent and endearing, conveying the feelings of the nation. The following section includes a collection of presidential quotes on citizenship and the important contributions of immigrants. As you read, note that throughout history, U.S. presidents have expressed a consistent message on these two themes.

GEORGE WASHINGTON

"The bosom of America is open to receive not only the Opulent and respectable Stranger, but the oppressed and persecuted of all Nations And Religions; whom we shall welcome to a participation of all our rights and privileges, if by decency and propriety of conduct they appear to merit the enjoyment." ★ 1783

President George Washington.
Courtesy of the Library of Congress,
LC-H824-T-P01-016

THOMAS JEFFERSON

"Born in other countries, yet believing you could be happy in this, our laws acknowledge, as they should do, your right to join us in society, conforming, as I doubt not you will do, to our established rules. That these rules shall be as equal as prudential considerations will admit, will certainly be the aim of our legislatures, general and particular." ★ 1801

President Thomas Jefferson.
Courtesy of the Independence National Historical
Park Collection, Philadelphia, PA

ABRAHAM LINCOLN

"Let us at all times remember that all American citizens are brothers of a common country, and should dwell together in the bonds of fraternal feeling." ★ 1860

ULYSSES S. GRANT

President Ulysses S. Grant.
Courtesy of the Library of Congress,
LC-USZ62-13018

"The immigrant is not a citizen of any State or Territory upon his arrival, but comes here to become a citizen of a great Republic, free to change his residence at will, to enjoy the blessings of a protecting Government, where all are equal before the law, and to add to the national wealth by his industry. On his arrival he does not know States or corporations, but confides implicitly in the protecting arm of the great, free country of which he has heard so much before leaving his native land." ★ 1872

"The United States wisely, freely, and liberally offers its citizenship to all who may come in good faith to reside within its limits on their complying with certain prescribed reasonable and simple formalities and conditions. Among the highest duties of the Government is that to afford firm, sufficient, and equal protection to all its citizens, whether native born or naturalized." ★ 1874

GROVER CLEVELAND

President Grover Cleveland.
Courtesy of the Library of Congress,
LC-USZ62-124416

"Heretofore we have welcomed all who came to us from other lands except those whose moral or physical condition or history threatened danger to our national welfare and safety. Relying upon the zealous watchfulness of our people to prevent injury to our political and social fabric, we have encouraged those coming from foreign countries to cast their lot with us and join in the development of our vast domain, securing in return a share in the blessings of American citizenship." ★ 1897

THEODORE ROOSEVELT

"The good citizen is the man who, whatever his wealth or his poverty, strives manfully to do his duty to himself, to his family, to his neighbor, to the State; who is incapable of the baseness which manifests itself either in arrogance or in envy, but who while demanding justice for himself is no less scrupulous to do justice to others. It is because the average citizen, rich or poor, is of just this type that we have cause for our profound faith in the future of the Republic." ★ 1903

President Theodore Roosevelt.
Courtesy of the Library of Congress, LC-USZ62-13026

"We are all of us Americans, and nothing else; we all have equal rights and equal obligations; we form part of one people, in the face of all other nations, paying allegiance only to one flag; and a wrong to any one of us is a wrong to all the rest of us."
★ 1917

Arriving in the United States.
Courtesy of the USCIS Historical Library

WOODROW WILSON

President Woodrow Wilson.
Courtesy of the Library of Congress,
LC-USZ62-107577

"This is the only country in the world which experiences this constant and repeated rebirth. Other countries depend upon the multiplication of their own native people. This country is constantly drinking strength out of new sources by the voluntary association with it of great bodies of strong men and forward-looking women out of other lands. And so by the gift of the free will of independent people it is being constantly renewed from generation to generation by the same process by which it was originally created....You have just taken an oath of allegiance to the United States. Of allegiance to whom? Of allegiance to no one, unless it is God—certainly not of allegiance to those who temporarily represent this great Government. You have taken an oath of allegiance to a great ideal, to a great body of principles, to a great hope of the human race." ★ 1915

"We came to America, either ourselves or in the persons of our ancestors, to better the ideals of men, to make them see finer things than they had seen before, to get rid of the things that divide and to make sure of the things that unite." ★ 1915

WARREN G. HARDING

"Nothing is more important to America than citizenship; there is more assurance of our future in the individual character of our citizens than in any proposal I, and all the wise advisers I can gather, can ever put into effect in Washington."
★ 1920

President Warren G. Harding.
Courtesy of the Library of Congress, LC-USZ62-106243

CALVIN COOLIDGE

President Calvin Coolidge.
Courtesy of the Library of Congress, ppmsc 03670

"*American citizenship is a high estate. He who holds it is the peer of kings. It has been secured only by untold toil and effort. It will be maintained by no other method. It demands the best that men and women have to give. But it likewise awards its partakers the best that there is on earth.*" ★ 1924

Asian immigrants arriving at Immigration Station on Angel Island near San Francisco, CA, 1931. Courtesy of the National Archives, College Park, MD

"*Whether one traces his Americanism back three centuries to the Mayflower, or three years to the steerage, is not half so important as whether his Americanism of today is real and genuine. No matter by what various crafts we came here, we are all now in the same boat.*" ★ 1925

FRANKLIN D. ROOSEVELT

"*The principle on which this country was founded and by which it has always been governed is that Americanism is a matter of the mind and heart; Americanism is not, and never was, a matter of race and ancestry. A good American is one who is loyal to this country and to our creed of liberty and democracy.*" ★ 1943

HARRY S. TRUMAN

"There is no more precious
possession today than
United States citizenship.
A nation is no stronger
than its citizenry. With
many problems facing us
daily in this perplexing
and trying era, it is vital
that we have a unity
of purpose—to the end
that freedom, justice,
and opportunity, good
will, and happiness may
be assured ourselves and
peoples everywhere."
★ 1948

President Harry S. Truman.
Courtesy of the Library of Congress, LC-USZ62-98170

JOHN F. KENNEDY

"Everywhere immigrants
have enriched and
strengthened the fabric
of American life."
★ 1959

Naturalization ceremony in
Milwaukee, WI, 1963.
Milwaukee Journal photo courtesy of the USCIS
Historical Library

Lyndon B. Johnson

"Our citizens—naturalized or native-born—must also seek to refresh and improve their knowledge of how our government operates under the Constitution and how they can participate in it. Only in this way can they assume the full responsibilities of citizenship and make our government more truly of, by, and for the people."

★ 1967

President Lyndon B. Johnson.
Courtesy of the Lyndon Baines Johnson Library and Museum

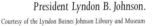

Ronald Reagan

President Ronald Reagan.
Courtesy of the Ronald Reagan Presidential Library

"It's long been my belief that America is a chosen place, a rich and fertile continent placed by some Divine Providence here between the two great oceans, and only those who really wanted to get here would get here. Only those who most yearned for freedom would make the terrible trek that it took to get here. America has drawn the stoutest hearts from every corner of the world, from every nation of the world. And that was lucky for America, because if it was going to endure and grow and protect its freedoms for 200 years, it was going to need stout hearts." ★ 1984

"I received a letter just before I left office from a man. I don't know why he chose to write it, but I'm glad he did. He wrote that you can go to live in France, but you can't become a Frenchman. You can go to live in Germany or Italy, but you can't become a German, an Italian. He went through Turkey, Greece, Japan and other countries. But he said anyone, from any corner of the world, can come to live in the United States and become an American." ★ 1990

GEORGE H. W. BUSH

"Nearly all Americans have ancestors who braved the oceans—liberty-loving risk takers in search of an ideal—the largest voluntary migrations in recorded history. Across the Pacific, across the Atlantic, they came from every point on the compass—many passing beneath the Statue of Liberty—with fear and vision, with sorrow and adventure, fleeing tyranny or terror, seeking haven, and all seeking hope...Immigration is not just a link to America's past; it's also a bridge to America's future." ★ 1990

President George H. W. Bush.
Courtesy of the George H. W. Bush Presidential Library

WILLIAM J. CLINTON

President William J. Clinton.
Courtesy of the William J. Clinton Presidential Library

"More than any other nation on Earth, America has constantly drawn strength and spirit from wave after wave of immigrants. In each generation, they have proved to be the most restless, the most adventurous, the most innovative, the most industrious of people. Bearing different memories, honoring different heritages, they have strengthened our economy, enriched our culture, renewed our promise of freedom and opportunity for all....And together, immigrants and citizens alike, let me say we must recommit ourselves to the general duties of citizenship. Not just immigrants, but every American should know what's in our Constitution and understand our shared history. Not just immigrants, but every American should participate in our democracy by voting, by volunteering and by running for office. Not just immigrants, but every American, on our campuses and in our communities, should serve—community service breeds good citizenship. And not just immigrants, but every American should reject identity politics that seeks to separate us, not bring us together." ★ 1998

GEORGE W. BUSH

President George W. Bush.
Official White House Photo

"*America has never been united by blood or birth or soil. We are bound by ideals that move us beyond our backgrounds, lift us above our interests and teach us what it means to be citizens. Every child must be taught these principles. Every citizen must uphold them. And every immigrant, by embracing these ideals, makes our country more, not less, American.*" ★ 2001

"*America's welcoming society is more than a cultural tradition, it is a fundamental promise of our democracy. Our Constitution does not limit citizenship by background or birth. Instead, our nation is bound together by a shared love of liberty and a conviction that all people are created with dignity and value. Through the generations, Americans have upheld that vision by welcoming new citizens from across the globe—and that has made us stand apart.*" ★ 2006

Naturalization ceremony
in San Diego, CA,
July 4, 2005.
Courtesy of the USCIS Office of
Communications

Prominent Foreign-Born Americans

Throughout our nation's history, foreign-born men and women have come to the United States, taken the Oath of Allegiance, and contributed greatly to their new communities and country. The United States welcomes individuals from nations near and far and immigrants have played an important role in establishing this country as the "land of opportunity." America takes great pride in being known as a "nation of immigrants."

The following section provides examples of individuals who have come to the United States, become citizens by choice, and left a lasting impression on our society. This list is by no means all encompassing, as a comprehensive record would be nearly impossible. Instead, it serves the purpose of highlighting a selection of foreign-born Americans, coming from a wide range of countries, who have had a significant impact on the United States as we know it today.

JOHN PAUL JONES (1747–1792)

American naval officer.
John Paul was born July 6, 1747, in Kirkbean, Kirkcudbrightshire, Scotland (now Dumfries and Galloway, Scotland). At age 21, he commanded his first ship and quickly became a very successful merchant skipper in the West Indies. In the mid 1770s, he moved to the British colonies in North America, adopting the last name "Jones." At the beginning of the American Revolution, he joined the Continental navy and was commissioned first lieutenant. During the

"John Paul Jones" by George Bagby Matthews.
Courtesy of the U.S. Senate

war, Jones commanded several vessels, including the *Duc de Duras*, which he renamed *Bon Homme Richard* in honor of Benjamin Franklin's *Poor Richard's Almanack*. Aboard this ship on September 23, 1779, Jones engaged the British vessel HMS *Serapis* off the coast of England. Jones defeated the HMS *Serapis* in one of the most storied battles in United States naval history. He is now entombed beneath the chapel of the

U.S. Naval Academy in Annapolis, Maryland.

The Bon Homme Richard.
Courtesy of the National Archives, NARA File # 019-N-10430

ALEXANDER HAMILTON (1757–1804)

First Secretary of the Treasury, serving under President George Washington. Hamilton was born January 11, 1757, on the island of Nevis, British West Indies (now part of the independent country of Saint Kitts and Nevis). Hamilton moved to America in 1772, where he attended preparatory school in Elizabethtown, New Jersey. At the outbreak of the American Revolution in 1776, Hamilton entered the Continental army in New York as captain of artillery. In 1777, he was appointed aide-de-camp to General George Washington. Hamilton was one of three men responsible for the *Federalist Papers*, and was a guiding spirit behind the adoption of the U.S. Constitution. With the adoption of the Constitution in 1787, Hamilton, like all other residents of the new nation, became an original "founding" citizen of the United States. He was also a founder and leader of the first political party in the United States, the Federalists.

WILLIAM A. LEIDESDORFF (1810–1848)

American businessman and first African American diplomat. Leidesdorff was born in the Danish West Indies (now the U.S. Virgin Islands) to a Danish man and an African woman in 1810. He was raised by a wealthy English plantation owner and obtained a formal education while in the Danish West Indies. Upon his caretaker's untimely death, he moved to the United States, settling in New Orleans, Louisiana. He became a naturalized U.S. citizen in 1834. Leidesdorff became active in the mercantile industry and soon developed a trade route between Yerba

William Leidesdorff.
Courtesy of the Virtual Museum of the City of San Francisco

Buena (now San Francisco), California, and Honolulu, Hawaii. In 1844, while living in California (then part of Mexico), he became a Mexican citizen in order to increase his landholdings. On October 29, 1845, Thomas O. Larkin, U.S. consul in Monterey, California, appointed Leidesdorff as vice consul at Yerba Buena. Leidesdorff secretly helped the United States annex the region of California. His service as vice consul lasted until the U.S. occupation of northern California in July 1846.

ALEXANDER GRAHAM BELL (1847–1922)

American inventor, introduced the telephone in 1876. Bell was born March 3, 1847, in Edinburgh, Scotland. In 1872, he moved to the United States, where he taught at Boston University. Bell became a naturalized U.S. citizen in 1882. At an early age, he was fascinated with the idea of transmitting speech. While working with his assistant, Thomas Watson, in Boston, Bell shared his idea of what would become the telephone. In 1876, Bell introduced the telephone to the world at the Centennial Exposition

Alexander Graham Bell.
Courtesy of the Library of Congress, LC-USZ62-14759

in Philadelphia, Pennsylvania. The invention of the telephone led to the organization of the Bell Telephone Company. Bell was also responsible for inventing the photophone in 1880, an instrument that transmitted

speech by light rays. In addition, he was a co-founder of the National Geographic Society, and served as its president from 1898 to 1904.

Alexander Graham Bell's first telephone.
Courtesy of the Library of Congress, LC-D420-2988

Joseph Pulitzer (1847–1911)

American newspaper publisher. Pulitzer was born April 10, 1847, in Makó, Hungary. He immigrated to the United States in 1864 to serve in the American Civil War, joining the First New York Cavalry. Pulitzer began his newspaper career as an employee of a German-language daily in St. Louis, Missouri. He became a naturalized U.S. citizen in 1867. After buying two St. Louis newspapers and merging them into the successful *St. Louis Post-Dispatch* in 1878, Pulitzer purchased the *New York World* in 1883. He shifted the newspaper's focus toward human-interest stories, scandals, and fighting corruption as the *World's* circulation grew from 15,000 to 600,000—the largest in the United States. Before his death in 1911, Pulitzer pledged money to set up a school of journalism at Columbia University in New York as well as the Pulitzer Prizes for journalists. The Pulitzer Prizes are now considered the most prestigious awards in print journalism.

Frances X. Cabrini (1850–1917)

American humanitarian and social worker, first U.S. citizen to be canonized by the Catholic Church. Cabrini was born July 15, 1850, in Sant'Angelo Lodigiano, Italy. After taking vows to become a nun in 1877, she began teaching at an orphanage in Codogno, Italy. In 1889, Pope Leo XIII sent her to New York to begin ministering to the growing number of new immigrants in the United States. She became a naturalized U.S. citizen in 1909. Throughout her lifetime, Cabrini worked with all those in need, including the poor, the uneducated, and the sick. She helped organize schools, orphanages, and adult education classes for immigrants in her nearly forty years of ministry. In 1946, Pope Pius XII canonized her, making her the first U.S. citizen to be canonized. Cabrini is now the Catholic Church's patron saint of immigrants.

Saint Frances Xavier Cabrini.
Courtesy of the Library of Congress, LC-USZ62-103568

MICHAEL PUPIN (1858–1935)

American physicist and inventor. Pupin was born October 4, 1858, in Idvor, Austria-Hungary (now Serbia). In 1874, he moved to the United States, settling in New York. Pupin graduated from Columbia University with a degree in physics in 1883. He became a naturalized U.S citizen that same year. In 1889,

Michael Pupin.
Public domain photo

Pupin obtained his doctorate from the University of Berlin. Upon graduation, he returned to Columbia University where he taught for more than forty years. Pupin was well known for his improvement of long-distance telephone and telegraph communication. Throughout his career, he received thirty-four patents for his inventions. In 1924, he won the Pulitzer Prize for his autobiography, *From Immigrant to Inventor*.

SOLOMON CARTER FULLER (1872–1953)

American psychiatrist, first known African American psychiatrist in the United States. Fuller was born in Monrovia, Liberia, in 1872. In 1889, he moved to the United States to attend Livingston College in Salisbury, North Carolina. He received his

Solomon Carter Fuller.
Courtesy of Boston University

M.D. from Boston University's School of Medicine in 1894, and began teaching there in 1899. Fuller spent a year in Munich, Germany, studying psychiatry. Much of his research centered on degenerative brain diseases including Alzheimer's disease, which he attributed to causes other than arteriosclerosis, a theory that was fully supported by medical researchers in 1953. Fuller became a naturalized U.S. citizen in 1920.

ALBERT EINSTEIN (1879–1955)

American scientist and Nobel laureate in physics, widely considered to be the greatest scientist of the twentieth century. Einstein was born March 14, 1879, at Ulm, in Württemberg, Germany. In 1921, he received the Nobel Prize in Physics for his discovery of the law of the photoelectric effect. Einstein's special theory of relativity containing the famous equation $E=mc^2$ also won him international praise. When the Nazis came to power in Germany in 1933, he immigrated to the United States and joined the newly formed Institute for Advanced Studies at Princeton University. Einstein became a naturalized U.S. citizen in 1940.

Albert Einstein receiving his certificate of American citizenship, October 1, 1940.

Courtesy of the Library of Congress, LC-DIG-ppmsca-05649

IGOR STRAVINSKY (1882–1971)

American composer. Stravinsky was born June 17, 1882, in
Oranienbaum, Russia (now Lomonosov, Russia). His early career was
spent composing in Switzerland and Paris, France. Stravinsky's works
include *The Rite of Spring* (1913), *The Soldier's Tale* (1918), *Oedipus Rex* (1927),
and *Perséphone* (1934). In 1939, he left Europe and settled in the United
States. Stravinsky became a naturalized U.S. citizen in 1945. The various
styles of music he experimented with made Stravinsky one of the most
influential composers of his time. He is now widely regarded as one of
the greatest composers of the twentieth century.

FELIX FRANKFURTER (1882–1965)

**American legal
scholar and U.S.
Supreme Court
Justice.** Frankfurter
was born November
15, 1882, in Vienna,
Austria-Hungary
(now Austria). In
1894, he immigrated
to the United States
and attended both
City College of New
York and Harvard Law
School. By virtue of
his father's natural-
ization, Frankfurter
became a naturalized
U.S. citizen. He went

Justice Felix Frankfurter.

on to serve as an assistant U.S. attorney in New York State (1906-1910) and a legal officer in the Bureau of Insular Affairs (1911-1914). From 1914 to 1939, Frankfurter was a professor at Harvard Law School. In 1939, President Franklin D. Roosevelt appointed him an associate justice to the U.S. Supreme Court.

KNUTE ROCKNE (1888–1931)

American football player and coach. Rockne was born March 4, 1888, in Voss, Norway. His father brought the family to the United States in 1893. By virtue of his father's naturalization, Rockne became a naturalized U.S. citizen in 1896. As the head football coach of the University of Notre Dame from 1918 to 1930, he achieved the greatest winning percentage of all time at .881 percent. During his years as head coach, Rockne collected 105 victories, twelve losses, five ties, and six national championships. He also coached Notre Dame to five undefeated seasons. Both as a player and a coach, Rockne popularized the use of the forward pass, which significantly changed how the game was played.

Knute Rockne, seated, at a Notre Dame football practice in the late 1920s.
Courtesy of the University of Notre Dame

IRVING BERLIN (1888–1989)

Irving Berlin.
Courtesy of the Library of Congress, LC-USZ62-37541

American composer and songwriter. Berlin was born May 11, 1888, in Mogilyov, Russia (now Belarus). In 1893, his family immigrated to the United States. He became a naturalized U.S. citizen in 1918. Berlin wrote music and lyrics for Broadway shows such as *Annie Get Your Gun* (1946) and *Miss Liberty* (1949), as well as for films such as *Holiday Inn* (1942), *Blue Skies* (1946), and *Easter Parade* (1948). He also wrote popular songs such as "There's No Business Like Show Business," "God Bless America," and the holiday classic "White Christmas." In 1955, President Dwight D. Eisenhower recognized Berlin's patriotic songs by presenting him with a special medal authorized by the U.S. Congress. In 1986, Berlin was one of twelve naturalized U.S. citizens to receive the Medal of Liberty from President Ronald Reagan.

FRANK CAPRA (1897–1991)

American film director and producer. Capra was born May 18, 1897, in Palermo, Italy. In 1903, his family immigrated to the United States, settling in Los Angeles. He became a naturalized U.S. citizen in 1920. Capra is known for directing such films as *Mr. Smith Goes to Washington* (1939), *It's a Wonderful Life* (1946), and *Mr. Deeds Goes to Town* (1936), for which he won the Academy Award for Best Director. Although it was considered a box office failure upon its release, his 1946 film *It's a Wonderful Life* has become one of the most beloved holiday films of all time.

DALIP SINGH SAUND (1899–1973)

American congressman and first Asian American to serve in the U.S. Congress. Saund was born September 20, 1899, in Chhajulwadi, Punjab, India. He graduated from the University of Punjab in 1919 and moved to the United States the following year to attend the University of California. Saund earned both a master's degree and a doctorate from the University of California. He then became a successful lettuce farmer in the Imperial Valley of California. He became a naturalized U.S. citizen in 1949. In 1952, Saund was elected judge of Justice Court for the Westmoreland Judicial District in California's Imperial County, a position he was

Dalip Singh Saund.
Courtesy of the Library of Congress, LC-USZ62-102603

denied two years earlier because he had not been a U.S. citizen for more than a year. In 1956, he was elected to represent the 29th Congressional District of California in the U.S. House of Representatives, becoming the first Asian American to serve in the U.S. Congress.

MARLENE DIETRICH (1901–1992)

American actress and singer. Dietrich was born December 27, 1901, in Berlin, Germany. She began her acting career in Berlin where she quickly became popular in the theater and in silent films. In 1929, she was cast in the film *The Blue Angel* (1930) by American director Josef von Sternberg. Her performance was widely acclaimed and Dietrich promptly moved to the United States. She starred in a variety of films during her career, including *Morocco* (1930), *The Devil Is a Woman* (1935), *Desire* (1936), and *Judgment at Nuremberg* (1961). She became a naturalized U.S. citizen in 1939. During World War II, Dietrich made over 500 appearances before American troops overseas.

BOB HOPE (1903–2003)

American entertainer. Hope was born May 29, 1903, in Eltham, Great Britain. In 1907, his father moved the family to Cleveland, Ohio. In 1920, by virtue of his father's naturalization, "Bob"—the name he took for the rest of his life—became a U.S. citizen. Throughout his career, he appeared in a variety of films and television specials, and performed many shows for American

Bob Hope.
Courtesy of the Bob Hope Collection

troops overseas, including World War II (1939–1945), the Korean War (1950–1953), the Vietnam War (1959–1975), and the Persian Gulf War (1991). In 1997, President William Clinton named him an honorary military veteran.

Subrahmanyan Chandrasekhar (1910–1995)

Subrahmanyan Chandrasekhar.
Courtesy of the University of Chicago

American scientist and Nobel laureate. Chandrasekhar was born October 19, 1910, in Lahore, India (now Pakistan). He earned a bachelor's degree in physics at Presidency College in Madras, India, and a doctorate from Trinity College in England. Chandrasekhar immigrated to the United States in 1937, where he joined the faculty of the University of Chicago. He became a naturalized U.S. citizen in 1953.

Chandrasekhar was the first to theorize that not all stars end up as white dwarf stars, but those retaining mass above a certain limit, known today as "Chandrasekhar's limit," undergo further collapse. In 1983, he was awarded the Nobel Prize in Physics for his theoretical studies of the physical processes important to the structure and evolution of stars. In 1999, the National Aeronautics and Space Administration (NASA) named one of its four "Great Observatories" orbiting the Earth in space for Chandrasekhar.

KENNETH B. CLARK (1914–2005)

American psychologist. Clark was born July 14, 1914, in the Panama Canal Zone. In 1919, he moved to the United States, settling in New York with his mother and sister. He became a naturalized U.S. citizen in 1931. Clark obtained a bachelor's degree from Howard University in 1935 and a master's degree in 1936. He went on to earn a doctorate in experimental psychology from Columbia University in 1940, becoming

Kenneth B. Clark.
Courtesy of the Library of Congress, LC-USZ62-115757

the first African American to earn a doctorate in psychology at the school. In 1946, he and his wife Mamie founded the Northside Center for Child Development in Harlem, New York, where they began conducting research on racial bias in education. A 1950 report from Clark on racial discrimination was cited in the landmark *Brown v. Board of Education* Supreme Court decision, which ruled public school segregation unconstitutional. Clark was also the first African American to serve as president of the American Psychological Association. In 1986, he was one of twelve naturalized U.S. citizens to receive the Medal of Liberty from President Ronald Reagan.

CELIA CRUZ (1925–2003)

Celia Cruz.
Courtesy of the Library of Congress, LC-USZ62-118256

American singer, known as the "Queen of Salsa." Cruz was born October 21, 1925, in Havana, Cuba. She became famous in Cuba in the 1950s, singing with the band La Sonora Matancera. Cruz left Cuba for the United States in 1960, after Fidel Castro came to power. She was soon headlining the Hollywood Palladium in California and Carnegie Hall in New York. Cruz became a naturalized U.S. citizen in 1961. She appeared in several films, including The Mambo Kings (1992) and The Perez Family (1995), and sang a duet with David Byrne for the 1986 film Something Wild. During her long career, Cruz received a Smithsonian Lifetime Achievement Award, a National Medal of the Arts, and honorary doctorates from Yale University and the University of Miami.

Naturalization ceremony in the Rotunda of the National Archives in Washington, DC, December 15, 2005.

Courtesy of the USCIS Office of Communications

Acknowledgements

U.S. CITIZENSHIP AND IMMIGRATION SERVICES AND THE OFFICE OF CITIZENSHIP would like to extend its appreciation to the following organizations for their support and assistance in the development of this publication:

CENTER FOR CIVIC EDUCATION
http://www.civiced.org

NATIONAL ENDOWMENT FOR THE HUMANITIES
http://www.neh.gov

NATIONAL CONSTITUTION CENTER
http://www.constitutioncenter.org

USCIS HISTORICAL REFERENCE LIBRARY
http://www.uscis.gov

MARILYN ZOIDIS,
formerly Senior Curator, Star-Spangled Banner Project,
Smithsonian Institution's National Museum of American History
http://americanhistory.si.edu

NATIONAL
ENDOWMENT
FOR THE
HUMANITIES

"Our nation is not bound together by common ties of blood, race, or religion; we are united instead by our devotion to shared ideals. So each generation of Americans—both native-born and immigrants—must learn our great founding principles, how our institutions came into being, how they work, and what our rights and responsibilities are. For this reason, the National Endowment for the Humanities is proud to support the development of **The Citizen's Almanac**. This valuable resource will help new Americans become educated and thoughtful citizens who can fully participate in our government of, by, and for the people."

— Bruce Cole, Chairman, National Endowment for the Humanities

Memories of the Occasion